Contents

This book is dedicated to my three children, Chloë,
Henry and Dannie, and my grandson Jace.

Introduction

Everyone gets anxious from time to time. Most people cope with it for the most part. A little anxiety can even, in some circumstances, be good. It can prompt you to act when action is needed. However, sometimes your anxiety can get out of control. Sometimes anxiety is too intense and stays for too long. It can become a bigger problem in your life than you would like. It can make you unhappy. It can make others around you unhappy.

This book is for anyone finding they can no longer control their anxiety. It is for those people who are finding that their anxiety is controlling them. By reading this book you will learn that anxiety takes many guises.

- A person can be a 'bag of nerves' during every waking moment.
- Or anxiety can be associated with a specific phobia, such as a fear of flying.
- There again, if you are compulsive about cleaning or checking, or if you think too much and worry, you are also showing signs of anxiety.

One of the first things to recognise is that anxiety can show itself in many different ways. Yet, strangely, a little anxiety can be good at times. It can be a prompt for action which can be of benefit to you. If you feel anxious about an event, such as preparing for a driving test, buying a house or leaving home for the first time, this can make you focus on a plan for success. However, when those first signs of anxiety do not lead to a good plan, when anxiety has no positive focus, things can get out of hand. Sustained levels of anxiety can make you ill or unhappy in a number of ways. Here are some examples of what anxiety can do to you. It can make you:

- Have disturbed sleep.
- Form bad habits, like drinking too much, which will affect your body and mind.
- Change your eating habits so you gain or lose too much weight.
- Develop strange fears or phobias or obsessions.
- Stressed and ill.

'Anxiety can show itself in many different ways.'

- Get at other people, nagging or blaming them unfairly.
- Mad at yourself.
- Feel vulnerable and like a loser.
- Focus on the wrong things in life.

Anxiety, therefore, can result in negative effects for your mind and body. Your personal and social life can suffer too if you cannot relate to people anymore in a calm and friendly way.

You can find yourself in a loop of despair. You might try to get better by seeking reassurance. Or, instead, you may avoid places you fear. Or you may blame yourself and totally lose your sense of self-esteem. Often, the very things you do to make your life better actually make things worse.

'Learn more about yourself and what matters to you.'

This book will help you understand the difference between the anxiety that we all feel at times and that can be a beneficial prompt to action, and anxiety that is damaging. It will help you understand your own anxiety problems. You will be guided to look in depth at the things in your life that are really getting to you and making you feel anxious and out of control. You will learn more about yourself and what matters to you. You will be guided to form a plan, to tackle your anxiety head on. The things you learn will stand you in good stead for any new and unexpected situations that may arise in your life. This book will give you the information necessary for you to make permanent changes for the good.

Disclaimer

This book provides general expert information and advice on anxiety and is not intended to replace specific medical advice from your own GP, but may be used alongside it. If your anxiety persists, you should consult your health care professional as soon as possible.

Chapter One

People Get Anxious

Anxiety is a word we all understand and are familiar with. To be anxious at times is completely normal. Through life people face challenges. These may be small and frequent anxieties, 'Can I get to work on time? Traffic is running so slowly'. Or the challenges may be less frequent, individual one-off events 'I have to make a speech at the wedding ... oh no!' Or the anxiety may be caused by challenges that are major life events, very stressful situations, such as divorce, illness, the children leaving home, buying a house, difficulties with people at work or with neighbours. Such events are likely to cause tension and high levels of anxiety.

Anxiety is there for a reason

Why do people react to events by feeling anxious? What is anxiety and what is its purpose? Once you think of an event as different and as threatening it is best for you to register it in some way. That is your survival instinct kicking in. Your body will automatically enter into a different physiological state:

- You will breathe more quickly.

- You will be energised for action.

- You will feel your heart pumping faster.

- You might start to sweat more.

- Your muscles will be primed and ready to go.

So this reaction can be very adaptive. If you see a car coming off the road and heading towards you, it is right you should feel immediate and high anxiety and your body should be primed sufficiently for you to throw yourself out of its path.

You can see from this example that to experience sudden anxiety can be a life-saving thing. Basically, anxiety can be good when it stimulates you to take appropriate action. Such action need not necessarily be related to a life-threatening event. Anxiety can, at times, be good and here are some examples:

- If your anxiety about making a speech at a wedding prompts you to ask around for ideas, to write out and practise your speech, that is a good thing.

- If you have an exam coming up and anxiety prompts you to make a revision plan and study, that is good.

- If anxiety about divorce is troubling you, that anxiety might prompt you to seek advice about your financial situation, your entitlements; you might seek to explore a different type of social life in the future.

You can see that these responses to anxiety are good, appropriate and adaptive if they lead to an action plan and goal that works for you and makes you happier.

- You feel anxious about something.

- You make a plan.

- You monitor how things are going.

- If they are not going quite as smoothly as you would like, you will start to feel anxious again and that anxiety can be the spur for making slight adjustments to your plan.

'Anxiety can be good when it stimulates you to take appropriate action.'

It could well take time and a number of changes to the plan to get to a goal that you are happy with. All of that procedure is a natural, almost universal way of coping with and controlling anxiety.

Sometimes your anxiety might be for someone else. You might worry about your partner or your children. Anxiety can be a sign you care. That is just great if that is the spur to get you helping out your loved ones when they need it. However, if you can't really help, or if you try to help and get nowhere, then your anxiety can increase. So then what can you do with all that anxiety making your life a misery? This book will help you find your answer.

Anxiety and denial

It is inadvisable not to acknowledge something as a threat when it actually is a threat. If you decide to deal with the upcoming exam by not thinking about it you might control anxiety short term, but long-term failure is going to lead to greater anxiety in the end. To take a more extreme example, if you decide to control anxiety about illness by ignoring that breast lump or that enlarging mole on your skin – if you use denial to cope with your immediate anxiety – that is going to work short term, but long term the effects could be serious illness and even premature death.

Where the anxiety reaction can go wrong

The physiological response, this feeling of anxiety and fear, can be appropriate. It is a safety mechanism designed to stimulate you to action to avoid potential danger.

However, it ceases to be appropriate if you learn to view small and safe events as dangerous. For example, if you are stressed and anxious about going out of the house, if you show high levels of anxiety-induced arousal on a daily basis by just thinking of going out, then that is going to seriously affect your health. You will be tense, anxious and unhappy at a fairly constant level. Your whole life will suffer if you feel so anxious about going out that you quit work and stop socialising away from home.

So, anxiety is a natural and unavoidable reaction to perceived threat. However, the important word in the sentence is 'perceived'. People who suffer from anxiety very often do not have an accurate perception of where threat really lies. They see threat where there is little or no threat present, where there is no need to feel anxiety to ensure survival.

'Anxiety ceases to be appropriate if you learn to view small and safe events as dangerous.'

Fear of flying

We all know that some people are extremely afraid of flying, so much so that they avoid travel by plane. Now, that might not make much difference to their life. If they have no desire to go abroad, if friends and family are happy to stay in their own country or travel by boat, that is fine. Coping by avoiding has worked to reduce anxiety in this particular case.

However, if they would like to travel, but their partner decides to fly abroad without them, going with friends instead, there is the potential for unhappiness to develop. Some people cope by using prescription drugs (or alcohol!) to get them over the flight and are happy to have these 'crutches'. But even drugs would not be sufficient to get some people on a plane.

It is possible to conquer such anxiety using psychological techniques. Ask someone who is afraid of flying what their thoughts are as they approach a plane and the chances are overwhelming that their cognitions are negative:

- 'What if it crashes?'
- 'Will we get there? Maybe not.'
- 'I can visualise us coming down in flames.'

Very often they rehearse in their minds news stories about plane crashes; but why do that? As it happens probabilities are overwhelming that the plane will not crash. You are more likely to get killed on the road on the way to the airport than in the plane (but both events are, of course, extremely unlikely). Why dwell, therefore, on the rare and unlikely event, why scare yourself unnecessarily?

It is possible to learn to re-evaluate your appraisals of threat, to develop different thoughts, to have different mental images. It is possible to conquer this anxiety as with other phobias.

Agoraphobia – fear of going out

Some people perceive the world outside of their front door as fraught with danger. They may worry about traffic, about feeling dizzy and falling over, about making a fool of themselves in front of others. As with the fear of flying, the thoughts and mental images associated with these fears are negative. A person with agoraphobia will see themselves falling or collapsing, or being in a traffic accident as a result of leaving the house. They perceive an unrealistic threat of danger and it prevents them from living a normal life.

In fact, there are not that many accidents inside the home and not that many outside either. Their perception is not a realistic one.

Common themes associated with phobias

In both of these examples there are common elements. People with these phobias assess the probability of disaster as unrealistically high. They avoid anxiety-provoking situations. Why do they do that? The simple answer is that they see disaster – at best looking a fool, at worst meeting a violent and untimely death – as associated with their feared activities. And the value, they put on life is, naturally, high. They assume that avoiding flying or staying indoors makes them safe.

Learning to assess probabilities more accurately and changing the thoughts and images in your mind, can be helpful in overcoming phobias. In addition, anxiety can be overcome by gentle, gradual approaches to the feared items over time. The positive benefits of going places and being more active can give pleasure. The positive spin-offs can lead to a more fulfilling life and the anxiety held in check.

You will be guided to give yourself small and manageable goals. Many people fail to overcome their anxiety because they try too hard, they plunge themselves into a frightening situation thinking that will help. This strategy is more likely to make things far worse.

Even more frightening for you is when a well-meaning friend assumes that to force you into a scary situation will help you overcome your phobia. Because they have no fear they cannot understand how anxious you are. Unfortunately, forcing someone to confront their feared situation too suddenly and in too extreme a way, is more likely to lead to friendship break-up than cure of the phobia.

Anxiety that is 'just there' most, or all, of the time

The thing about perceiving a threat, or having a phobia, is that you at least think you can see what the problem is. You have an idea of what is frightening you, and if that thing is there, if you avoid it, you feel in control of one aspect of your anxiety.

However, for some people the anxiety-provoking problem cannot be avoided. If you are stressed at work, by people, by your boss or by too heavy a workload, you feel pressure and a level of anxiety for much of the time. You might feel stressed during the day but also feel anxious at night, waking worried from your sleep. Such anxiety has encroached on your life outside of work and made you very unhappy.

Perhaps you get anxious about little things:

- If someone makes a comment you might see it as criticism and worry you have done something wrong.

- You think about it over and over again, you ruminate.

- The worry stays with you and, if anything, gets worse.

- Have you really done something wrong?

- Have you upset someone?

- Is something bad going to happen now?

- Are people going to think badly of you?

- Do you feel guilty?

Such thoughts play round and round your head, in what feels like a completely uncontrollable way.

If you are anxious about your marriage, your children, your job prospects, your financial situation, that can lead to continued levels of stress and anxiety. You know what the problem is but it seems insurmountable. Or you know it might be solved in the fullness of time, but for the foreseeable future you are stuck with your worries and your anxieties. Nothing can be done and you feel sick with anxiety.

There again, life might be okay. Nothing brilliant is happening but there are no potential disasters on the horizon either, at least as far as you can see, yet you feel anxious. You have a sense of dread and foreboding. You may feel anxious but not know why. You may even feel a bit depressed with it.

Or, you may have a large range of all sorts of anxiety-provoking thoughts. If it is possible to worry about anything, you will, and those anxieties might relate to any number of things:

- 'Are the children safe?'

- 'Will my partner lose their job?'

- 'Have I saved enough for the future?'

- 'What if I get ill?'

- 'What if this cough means I have lung cancer?'

- 'Nothing good is happening, I am getting older, what have I achieved with my life? I feel anxious most of the time and worried about the future but goodness only knows why.'

Worrying about safety and feeling responsible

Sometimes anxiety manifests itself in behaviour patterns that relate to safety and security. It can feel important to get things 'just right' absolutely all the time.

This is different from being appropriately careful and liking things to be orderly. Those things can be good and very helpful, particularly in certain situations or certain professions. For instance, if you visit a dentist I am sure you will want to see someone who is scrupulously clean and meticulous in the way they carry out their work. It would not do for a heart surgeon to be 'slap dash' in their approach to the operations they perform. To be successful in many professions, such as being an architect, a decorator, a landscape gardener, a GP or a dentist, requires an orderly and meticulous approach to work.

So, to like order and an appropriate level of cleanliness is not necessarily a bad thing. However, with some anxiety disorders this gets out of hand. If a person cleans their hands over and over again until their skin is raw and bleeding, it is maladaptive and harmful. If a person checks that a light is off, or the gas is off, dozens of times through the day in a ritualistic manner, those actions are obviously unhelpful. No matter how much they check they cannot relax, cannot believe that all is actually well.

Some anxieties related to harm can result in repetition of safety behaviour performed to reduce tension. One repetition dissipates the worry but only for a very brief and temporary moment; so the safety behaviour has to be performed again, and again and again. The person never has the chance to learn that 'leaving it' does not result in disaster.

Being anxious around other people

Some people experience anxiety in social situations or in crowds. They may feel unsafe going out alone and choose not to go out unless they are with somebody that they know and trust. There again, others are happy to do this but feel anxious if they have to talk to a stranger, to go into a shop. They feel people are looking at them, judging them. They feel susceptible to criticism, for example:

- 'I am being looked at because I am too fat.'
- 'People are looking at me because I look ugly.'
- 'I am different from others and I will be mocked.'

More commonly, people adjust to being in the presence of others but in a social situation which calls for different or unusual activity such as going for an interview or giving a speech, they feel high anxiety that is difficult to cope with.

Panic reactions

A feeling of anxiety can be of sudden onset and brief, or it can be all pervasive. It can result in ritualised behaviour sometimes. It can be associated with a particular feared object or event, or it can be general. It takes many guises.

Irrespective of type of anxiety, some people find themselves victims of panic. The panic can be associated with their fear (of flying, of open spaces, of a phobic stimulus) or sometimes a panic attack can seem to come on for no known reason.

Panic attacks can happen out of the blue. Often the symptoms of a panic attack, such as difficulty drawing breath, rapid pulse and feeling faint, can mimic a heart attack.

It is important, when learning to control and conquer anxiety, to be aware of the body's responses to anxiety, to learn to recognise the symptoms that anxiety can bring, and to learn to control the panic and feel in control of your body once again.

Why you get stuck with anxiety

As I mentioned earlier in this chapter, sometimes anxiety can be good if it stimulates you to do something positive about a problem, to get things right. Your anxiety stimulates you to prepare for the exam and you do well. You practise the wedding speech and it is well received.

However, what people do to control their anxiety very often makes it worse or makes it stick. It stays with them and will not go away.

'What people do to control their anxiety very often makes it worse'

Here are some of the things that people typically do to get rid of their anxiety:

- They avoid the thing they are scared of.

- They adapt their lifestyle so they never have to confront their feared object or feared situation.

- They seek repeated, often daily, reassurance from friends or relatives, 'Will I be alright do you think?', 'Did I lock that door before we left?'.

- They seek reassurance from the medical profession, not just once, but again and again. A headache might be a brain tumor. The cough might be cancer. Is their blood pressure too high? Did they feel a heart murmur?

- They develop safety behaviour, like repeated checking or washing.

- They seek order – things in straight lines, in particular patterns.

- They have little things they say to themselves, such as prayers or recitations.

- They have rituals, like avoiding certain numbers; or they may have favourite numbers.

- They may wear particular clothes, the 'lucky outfit', or have items that keep them 'safe'.

- They become over reliant on prescription drugs to keep calm. They may adapt to them so they are less effective; so they take more, possibly becoming addicted.

- They drink too much alcohol.

- They decide to focus and control something in their life. They might, for instance, decide to have a particular and restricted way of eating. Or they might just eat lots and lots for comfort.

- They might get at someone else – become a nag – rather than focus on the real cause of their anxiety.

- They might call an ambulance or go to A&E on numerous occasions because they think they are having a heart attack.

- They might go over their problem, replay a scene they are worried about, over and over again in their mind.

'You can learn to stop unhelpful rumination. You need goals which help you gain a new perspective, a new focus.'

Now it is very unlikely indeed you will have adopted all of these strategies to cope with your particular anxiety. However, if you have been anxious for some time and the anxiety has stayed at the same level or become worse, it is probable that you have adopted at least one of these strategies. You are most likely avoiding, or seeking reassurance, or possibly you might be anxious about something that is simply unavoidable but you go over and over it in your mind replaying disaster or imagining the most terrible outcomes.

You can learn to stop unhelpful rumination. You need goals which help you gain a new perspective, a new focus. You may need to learn to relax more and accept that in everyday life there will be some risk; some things are not controllable and you have to learn to accept that and not ruin your life with constant worry.

Get ready to take action

The aim of this book is to give you knowledge about all the various facets of the problem that we call anxiety. Anxiety can show itself in so many ways and to start with it is essential for you to consider just what your particular anxiety is, what your fears are. You will need to think about what your current strategies are for controlling anxiety. Maybe you are doing something that is keeping the anxiety alive. You will be guided to consider what functions your anxiety and your anxiety-related behaviour have for you. In other words, you will be taking a really good look at yourself, your life and what your anxiety problem actually is.

Once you can clearly describe your problem you can also look at the factors that surround it:

- What makes that anxious feeling start?
- What effects do you experience in terms of thoughts, feelings and emotions?
- How does your body feel when anxious?
- What do you do to control your anxiety?
- Do you involve other people in this, and if so, who do you approach? What do you say? What is their reaction?

Next you will be shown how to draw up a plan of action. If curing anxiety was easy you would have done it by now. But that has not happened, despite your best efforts you remain anxious. You may even have other problems as well, for example, you may be depressed and feel down. Or you may feel life is at an all-time low, you may be unhealthy because you are not eating, drinking and sleeping in an appropriate way. You may be having problems at your work or in your home life.

Any good plan will include steps that lead to solutions to your particular problems. What can you do to make the anxiety go away? How should you behave differently? What thoughts are more appropriate? How can you learn to think differently, to control your mind? How can you relax and avoid a panic attack? How can you feel safe without going through your rituals, seeking reassurance or avoiding things?

This book will help you develop a plan to tackle all your anxieties and it will serve as a guide to ensure that you have a less anxious future. You will be happier. Those around you will be happier. It is all well and good for you to try to pull yourself together, to snap out of it. However, if it was that easy to cure anxiety you would have done it by now. You need a guide, and this book will serve as your guide.

How to help yourself to a less anxious future

As it happens, there is now scientific evidence that relates to the best types of methods to cure anxiety problems. You can learn to change your thoughts. Most people believe that their thoughts are spontaneous and uncontrollable, but that is far from the case. You can learn to change the way you think and that will change your emotions too. Thoughts, emotions, the way you behave, are all related and you can learn to understand the relationship between these. You can learn to reduce your anxiety and be able to cope with situations in life that provoke anxiety. What you learn by reading this book will help you overcome anxiety now and in the future.

'You can learn to change the way you think and that will change your emotions too.'

Summing Up

Everybody gets anxious from time to time. If it is a temporary thing, a spur to action, it can be good. However, anxiety can go on too long. It can sometimes not be a spur to action. It can sit with you. It can make you unhappy in all sorts of ways. The things you do to make anxiety go away can actually make it stay. To understand what is really making you anxious is a good start. You can go on to see if your attitude to your anxiety is making it worse. Then you can learn to tackle it head on.

Chapter Two

Anxiety Has Many Disguises

Thoughts and feelings that are part of anxiety

When you have anxiety it is sometimes obvious to you. If your anxiety levels are very high it will be obvious to others too. You think, act and look worried. With extreme anxiety you may start to sweat or tremble or breathe heavily as your anxiety grows into major fear. Your anxiety might crop up unexpectedly for no reason and you worry or even have a major panic attack.

Or anxiety can be there in the background most of the time. You might know why it is there, you might be able to name the thing or the person that is making you anxious. Or sometimes it just sits with you, making you a lot less happy than you should be. Here are some of the typical feelings and thoughts that accompany anxiety:

▪ A sick feeling in your stomach, like 'butterflies'.

▪ Dizziness or a feeling you are going to fall.

▪ Sweating or trembling.

▪ Finding it difficult to breathe.

▪ Finding it hard to swallow or to get words out.

▪ Rapid heart rate that feels like a heart attack might be starting.

▪ Pacing around or feeling you can't settle.

▪ Being short-tempered with others.

- Feeling that you are not good enough.

- Dreading failure.

- Foreseeing disaster.

- Feeling vulnerable or unsafe.

- Feeling responsible for others, but never sure you can keep them safe enough.

- Worrying you will make a fool of yourself.

- Worrying you will let others down.

- Feeling you are going to die.

- Feeling things are unreal.

With anxiety it is possible to have a mixture of such things. Sometimes you live with anxiety so long that you just assume these feelings and thoughts are part of you and fixed forever. They are not. They are part of your anxiety and they can be changed. You can learn to change them. You will find if you are anxious that you will almost certainly be making two wrong assumptions:

- You will think things are more threatening than they actually are. That is to say, you will overestimate how dangerous things are.

- You will think you cannot cope as well as you can. That is, you will underestimate your ability to deal with threat.

You can see how unfortunate it is that people who suffer from anxiety hold both assumptions. It is no wonder that if you think these two thoughts you are going to be living a far more unhappy life than you should. You see danger, and you think you are not strong enough to cope. In reality, things are not as bad as they seem and, in fact, you have the resources to deal with them. You have to change your pattern of thinking to help you overcome your anxiety.

Types of anxiety

Different types of anxiety are, together, sometimes called the 'anxiety disorders'. In fact, they are so common that you will find that at least one of these descriptions applies to you or someone you know. Calling the anxiety a 'disorder' is simply a helpful way to describe some of the types of anxiety that a great many people have. Some people have the disorder to a mild extent, some have it more severely.

Obsessive-compulsive disorder

Sometimes people like things to be tidy or are very careful and that can be a useful thing. Their personality might be described as rather obsessional but that does not mean they have obsessive-compulsive disorder (sometimes known as OCD). The disorder can be very debilitating. Sometimes the person has severe anxiety about thoughts in their head. They worry, they ruminate over and over about a situation and this leads to high anxiety. Here are some of the typical obsessional thoughts that might trouble a person with OCD:

- 'Is this clean enough for me to be safe and will my loved ones be safe?'

- 'Did I turn the light off, or the gas off, or did I lock the door?'

- 'What if I accidently hurt someone? I might push someone by mistake into the road or onto a train track without realising it.'

- 'Am I safe enough? What if I get cancer because I have not cleaned enough or I have been with people that might give me a disease?'

Such thoughts can be with a person with OCD every day. Such thoughts can trigger enormous anxiety. The person with OCD often feels highly responsible for ensuring safety. They would feel guilty if anything went wrong.

Rather than just telling themselves that these are only thoughts, just words going round inside their head, the typical person with OCD tries to get rid of the anxiety by performing compulsive acts or rituals that dissolve the anxiety. Here are some examples of things people with OCD do to get rid of anxiety:

- Cleaning over and over and over again. This might involve hand washing or cleaning other things.

- Checking and rechecking, for example, that gas or electric is off, or that the door is locked.

- Straightening things and keeping things in rigid order.

- Avoiding places where they might hurt or bump into others.

- Asking family members to lock away things like cleaning products in case they accidently poison people, for example, by adding bleach to food.

- Keeping themselves safe by having a mantra in their head, for example, they might count, or they might say a prayer.

- Seeking reassurance, 'Am I safe?', 'Did I lock the door?' from family or others.

Although such compulsions make the anxiety go away when the compulsive ritual is being carried out, it returns very quickly afterwards. So the person repeats the compulsive behaviour again and again and again. They never give themselves the chance to learn that if they did nothing, the anxiety would slowly ebb away all by itself. The dreaded event does not happen even though they have not completed their ritual. The person with OCD never learns that, in fact, they are imagining a danger that is not there.

People with severe OCD have their lives taken over by their anxiety. Often they spend so much of every day performing their rituals that they have no time for going out working or socialising. Their life becomes limited and often their home becomes a prison of their own making.

Phobias

All of us have things we like more than others. We learn to dislike some objects or situations intensely. Some of the dislikes that you learn may develop into a fear of a particular activity or object. We then say you are phobic about that thing. You have a phobia.

Phobias are, for the most part, conditioned learning experiences. It would seem that some objects more readily promote unease than others. Generally, it is thought that human beings are more likely to develop conditioned fear to certain objects rather than others. For example, you hear of many people with a fear of snakes or spiders, but hardly anyone has a fear of pencils or tables. Some things seem, naturally, to strike us as potentially more dangerous than others. Therefore they are more likely to develop into phobias than others. Such things are those which potentially seem more painful or threatening.

Yet we do not all develop phobias of, say, spiders or snakes or needles to give injections that are painful; so why is that? It is due to our learning experiences.

For example, if you hear that it is painful to have an injection, and then in the clinic as a young child you see babies crying after their injection, you will be alert to potential pain and danger. If, when the needle goes in your arm, you do indeed feel it go in, perhaps see some blood, you are probably not going to like it. Most young children get over this, the nurse says some soothing things, the parent says not to worry it will soon be alright, and the pain is quickly forgotten. You can learn to tolerate some degree of short-term discomfort for long-term protection.

However, if you are not comforted enough, or if your parent also shows fear, you will start to see danger and you have the makings of a potential phobia of needles. If the painful episode is talked about and rehearsed, if you are described as a fearful child, you might actually start thinking you are really afraid of needles, you will become fearful or phobic of them.

There again, you might, at any age, have a very painful experience (for example, in a hospital or at the dentist) and that will make you fearful or promote development of a phobia. Or you might see something that affects you badly, for example, the death of a loved one in hospital, and thereafter you become phobic of the sights, sounds and smells associated with hospitals.

Agoraphobia

Without experiencing direct pain you might imagine potential pain or even death, 'If the car crashes I could be injured for life', 'If I go outdoors I might get run over'. Think these thoughts enough and you could become afraid, stay at home all the time, become agoraphobic. Although you will be safe from being run over by a car, your life is likely to be less happy because you are not being sociable or cannot go out to work.

Social phobia

People want to be liked and even very solitary characters live in a world where some kind of social interaction is virtually inevitable.

▪ But what if you have been laughed at?

- What if, as a child, you never had the opportunity to interact with the other children much?

- What if you were the outsider?

- What if you worry about your looks?

- What if you think you are too fat? Or too thin?

- What if you wear glasses and you hate them?

- What if you have been called names because of the way you look?

- What if you have tried to talk to people but they looked bored with you?

- What if you feel you do not have what it takes to be one of the 'in crowd'?

It is very easy to end up feeling dejected and giving up. You lose self-esteem. You feel that people are looking at you. All your confidence in social situations goes and you start keeping out of people's way.

Two important points to realise about phobias:

- You learnt to have this phobia, and so you can unlearn it and become free.

- To avoid the thing you are afraid of will not help you overcome your fear.

'To avoid the thing you are afraid of will not help you overcome your fear'

Generalised anxiety disorder

Sometimes you just don't know what is worrying you. Yet when you wake, you feel anxious, you are worried. That feeling goes on day after day, it can last months and for many people it can last years, this is known as generalised anxiety disorder (GAD).

Quite often this kind of anxiety comes along when life just isn't going right. Maybe you are not as busy as you were. There is no job to take your mind off things. You don't have a single big worry. Your children are doing alright, although they may have left home and be forging a life for themselves elsewhere. Yet you cannot just relax and let yourself be happy. There is always something to worry about somewhere. If nothing bad is happening at the moment you worry about what if something bad does come along. 'What if the ceiling caves in?', 'What if an accident should happen?', 'What if I become ill?'. You might find you're just anxious all the time.

Some people with GAD almost wish they did have a focus for their worry, and then they could do something about it. People with GAD just feel helpless. If they think about how to be happier they can come up with no solutions. Quite often people with GAD describe themselves as being in something of a rut:

- They have no job or the job is boring.

- Their relationship is alright but predictable, monotonous.

- They feel unwanted. No one needs them.

- Life is a slow drag from day to day.

There is no focus for some happy thoughts. In effect, the good times have come and gone and there is precious little to look forward to. It is just a case of surviving from day to day and getting through life as best they can.

Health anxiety

We are bombarded with information about how to be healthy:

- Do not smoke cigarettes, and if you do, give them up.

- Do not drink too much alcohol.

- Eat in a healthy way.

- Exercise more.

- Get your weight under control.

- Do not use sunbeds.

- Use a sunscreen.

- Go to your GP if you find you have a lump on your body.

- See your GP if your bowel habits change.

- See your GP if you have a persistent cough.

It is therefore not surprising that people start to see these messages and become aware of their body, their habits.

For the most part this is a good thing. If you deny you have a problem and do not seek help sometimes serious illness can develop. To get checked out is advisable. Nine times out of 10 there will not be a problem, but if there is a problem, early detection can often lead to cure.

If you listen to the health messages and decide to lose a bit of weight, change diet, give up smoking, drink less, it is all to the good.

However, for some people the messages to get healthy get blown out of all proportion. They start worrying about every tiny little ache and pain. They turn up with a standard headache to their GP, thinking it is a life-threatening growth in the brain. A slight stomach upset is thought of as stomach cancer. Or they might obsess about food, refusing to eat anything with saturated fat, thinking of a cake or chips as somehow lethal.

Health anxiety can lead to repeated trips to the GP, requests for referral for scans and X-rays. You might think that if tests come back and give the 'all clear' the person would feel reassured. Normally that is what would happen. That would be the end of it. Life would resume as normal.

'When reassurance is given, anxiety goes away for only a short time and then it starts up again.'

However, for a person with health anxiety the reassurance lasts for an hour, a day, a week or so. Then worries resume. 'What if the test was inaccurate?' 'What if that problem has gone but there is another one developing?' Then they seek reassurance from friends or relatives, and often their GP. This becomes the pattern of their life.

There are some important factors to note here:

- Once a person becomes worried about health, they seek reassurance.

- When the reassurance is given, their anxiety goes away for only a short time, and then it starts up again.

In fact the reassurance is all part of the cycle. You worry, you get reassurance. For a short time you feel good. Then you worry again. So you seek reassurance. So on it goes.

Panic disorder

Panic disorder is interesting in that, rather than having a phobia, or having a general anxiety about things, or having OCD, or a worry about health, you just have strange attacks of panic that come on suddenly. You might not have any idea why you have them. You can be walking along a road, or sat at home watching television, and then out of the blue it strikes. You will start feeling hot, sweaty, your heart will be beating really fast and you might have trouble getting your breath. You might think 'This is it, I am going to die'. And with that thought you will, naturally, begin to panic even more.

People who have panic attacks say there is really nothing worse. You feel like you are dying. It is unimaginable fear.

Such attacks can last a few minutes or more. Someone having a panic attack might well call an ambulance; death seems just around the corner after all. If you are on a train or plane or outdoors somewhere, think how much worse the panic attack might be. You will start worrying about whether an ambulance can get to you in time.

In fact, the symptoms of a panic attack can very closely mimic the symptoms of a heart attack. This, of course, is likely to make you panic more. As you panic your body pumps adrenalin, your heart beats faster. You start gasping at the air. You then start getting dizzy because you have breathed in too much oxygen. That makes you think you are really going to die this time. You get stuck in a vicious circle.

This is why, when a person with a panic attack attends an A&E department of a hospital, they may be asked to breathe in and out of a bag. You re-breathe your own air back in. This air from the bag then becomes less full of oxygen. You carry on breathing it. There is less oxygen in the air in the bag with every breath you take. Therefore you stop being so giddy. You return to normal. You feel that happening and the panic subsides.

'The symptoms of a panic attack can very closely mimic the symptoms of a heart attack. This, of course, is likely to make you panic more.'

Panic attacks can happen with most kinds of anxiety

Panic attacks can occur like this and some people have no other anxiety problems apart from the panic. They have panic disorder.

However, panic is part of many of the other anxiety disorders. You can panic and have a full blown panic attack if you are frightened enough. If you have a phobia about flying or going on a train you can have a panic attack once you are on the plane or train. If you are agoraphobic, frightened of going outdoors, you can have a panic attack at the end of your own road.

You can see that feelings of panic are part of the anxiety disorders. They can be mild feelings of panic or they can get blown up into full panic attacks.

Stress caused by a trauma

Most people have heard of stress caused by a trauma, sometimes called post-traumatic stress disorder (PTSD). Often you think of it as associated with major events, like war or observing a death. Soldiers may get PTSD and suffer from it when they return home from war. They get mental images, flashbacks, of the terrible things they have seen.

Or if someone has survived a car accident they can have flashbacks of the accident. Life-threatening and violent events are most often associated with PTSD.

However, sometimes even people living more everyday lives can suffer from PTSD. Children can suffer from the trauma of having their parents divorce. A key negative event can be experienced as a major trauma in anyone's life, you do not need to have gone to war or have witnessed death to suffer a major trauma.

There are certain defining features of PTSD:

- People try to avoid the place or the thing that is associated with the trauma.

- Mood changes – people with PTSD feel very low, almost numb. They cannot feel involved in life in the way they did before.

- PTSD can make people irritable. They get at people. Nothing is right.

- Concentration can be difficult. People with PTSD often find it difficult to settle to doing things.

Other things that can go wrong

You might suffer from any kind of anxiety disorder and find that you start behaving in a way that makes things worse:

- You can become argumentative.

- You can be unhelpful to people.

- You start finding fault in others for little reason.

- You start finding fault with yourself.

- You cry a lot.

- You drink too much.

- You stop eating, or you might eat lots.

- You stop looking after yourself.

- You stop caring about your appearance.

- Or you start trying to fix your appearance, by surgery or fancy face creams or expensive cosmetic dentistry.

- You go shopping and spend too much.

- You have an affair just to prove a point to your partner.

- You self-harm.

- You put people down as that will make you look good in comparison.

In short, there are a great many things that can result from anxiety. It can develop into depression, strange social and behavioural patterns. Anxiety affects different people in different ways. You might find you have certain things you think, feel and do as a result of your anxiety. You will be guided to spot these patterns, to understand the full extent of your anxiety. Then you will be able to start to tackle your problem and turn your life around.

Summing Up

Anxiety is a single word that is used to describe a multitude of different problems. There are the anxiety disorders, but as well as these are lots of different problems that can sit alongside anxiety. You can be anxious about a great many things. Your anxiety can make you behave in strange ways. However, there are some things that most anxious people do. They avoid the thing that makes them anxious and they seek reassurance from others. Both of these things tend to make anxiety worse. Anxious people see things as more threatening than they really are. Then they underestimate their own ability to cope should things go wrong. Their thoughts and their behaviour fuel their anxiety rather than getting rid of it.

Chapter Three

Your Own Anxiety

Paint a picture of your situation

As you read the last chapter you will be able to spot if your anxiety falls into a particular category of disorder. Or you might find you have anxieties that fall into a number of anxiety groupings.

You might be able to say what your anxiety is about in terms of a specific disorder. You should know if it is general, or if it is associated with a named fear or phobia, or if you have OCD or panic disorder, or maybe even PTSD.

Even if you are unsure and your anxiety does not fit neatly into a single description of a disorder, you will be able to reflect on your own situation:

- When did it start?
- Why did it start?
- What is troubling you the most?
- Who do you worry about?
- What do you worry about?
- When you worry, how do you feel physically? And what sort of thoughts run through your head?
- Who do you turn to when you are anxious?
- What eating or drinking or other habits are associated with your worry?
- Do you get depressed because you can't cope with your anxiety?
- Is there anything else you can think of that is directly related to your anxiety?

- Do you blame a particular person for your anxiety?

- Do you put your anxiety down to a particular event?

At this point it will be useful for you to think carefully about all these things. In the next chapter you will be shown how to reflect more on your situation and to keep useful notes as you learn to become your own therapist. But here you are aiming to get in your mind as full a description as you can of your anxiety problem as it exists for you now in your day-to-day life. Consider these issues also:

- Do you think things are dangerous?

- What is dangerous and why is it dangerous?

- Do other people get as anxious as you about these things?

- Do you tend to see danger where there is none? Or do you generally view things as a threat much more than other people? Is this realistic of you?

- Do you think you could not cope if things went wrong?

You might like to know that people who are highly anxious still cope pretty well if something goes wrong. Even if the worst happens you have the capacity to overcome, to learn to come to terms with life events. If you suffer from anxiety you will be pleased to know that you have more ability to cope with disaster than you think you have.

Think about how you view yourself:

- Do you feel responsible for other people's safety? In what ways?

- Why do you feel this way?

- Would you feel guilty if things went wrong and if so, why?

Think about the things you do to keep anxiety at bay:

- What do you do when anxiety arises?

- How do you behave?

- Do you seek reassurance?

- Who do you seek reassurance from?

- How long does the feeling of safety last before anxiety starts back?

Think about what your anxiety is doing to your life:

- Is there anything it is preventing you from doing?
- Does it make you behave in ways that make you miserable?
- Does it make you behave in ways that take up too much of your time?
- In what ways is anxiety ruining your life?
- In what ways is your anxiety making other people's lives difficult?

Are you feeling stuck with your anxiety? Most people who have been anxious for a long time would much prefer not to be this way. However, if you wake up anxious every day it is difficult to pull yourself out of the situation. Your problem can be difficult to deal with if you do not break it down into manageable parts. You cannot 'think' yourself out of anxiety just by telling yourself to snap out of it.

It is only by looking at the details of your problem, by thinking about your feelings, the thoughts that run through your head, the habits that go hand in hand with anxiety, that you can learn to change.

This is just the beginning of your learning experience. As you progress through this book you will be going into more depth about the issues that you have started to consider here.

Where does anxiety begin?

Some people think that, to tackle anxiety, you have to understand how it arose in the first place. Sometimes this is easy to spot and sometimes it is impossible to know. Really, it does not matter. Even if you never understand what caused your anxiety you can still learn to overcome it.

It might be that you come from a family where there were lots of concerns expressed. If your parents thought life was full of danger then they may have inadvertently made you more wary than you should be. But that does not matter. Irrespective of your background, you can learn to take a fresh view of your life now.

You might like to know, however, that anxiety is often associated with key events that can turn up in anyone's life. Here are some of the life events that can trigger anxiety:

'Even if you never understand what caused your anxiety you can still learn to overcome it.'

- Death of a loved one.

- Severe illness that might threaten your own life or the life of a loved one.

- Injury or illness, especially if it is severe enough that it is unlikely that good health will ever come back.

- Divorce.

- Separation from a partner, in fact any separation from loved ones (such as children leaving home).

- Getting married or civil partnership.

- Moving house.

- Moving out of your family home and starting a new life elsewhere.

- New life – pregnancy.

- Changing jobs and things associated with that, such as redundancy.

- Retirement.

'Events that happen bring unpredictable consequences and you will have to adapt to them. You will need to feel you have control of the new situation.'

You will see from this list that a cause of anxiety is major life change. Divorce or death of a loved one can be awful and so it's no surprise that you will become anxious. However, moving to a lovely new house, or the birth of a baby, are usually happy events but they too can cause anxiety. This is because any event which causes change will be something you will need to adapt to.

Your life will alter in unusual and often unpredictable ways. You might imagine how life will be but you will not be completely right. There may be shocks. For example, you move house and discover your neighbours are a nightmare. There may be financial strain associated with an expensive mortgage. If you are a mother some events, like the birth of a baby, will have physical and hormonal effects on you. So, despite the fact you are thrilled with the new arrival, your body has stretch marks and you have weight you cannot shift. You miss your friends at work and experience broken sleep.

Events that happen bring unpredictable consequences and you will have to adapt to them. You will need to feel you have control of the new situation. Or, if control is not possible, you have to learn to accept it. If a loved one dies you cannot bring them back. If you develop a terminal illness, when you hear about it your anxiety levels will soar. But there comes a time when, to control anxiety, you have to learn to accept the situation and make the most of the present time, every precious moment. Cherish your happy memories and be grateful for them.

How does anxiety get worse?

Anxiety usually will go away as time moves on. You learn to act in such a way you get over your problems.

- If you divorce, you find new friends or get married again.

- If you move, you eventually settle down in the new neighbourhood.

- Your children move away but do visit occasionally and also you develop new social activities.

- Your new baby starts to sleep at night after a while.

- You find a new job or get some hobbies to fill your free time.

- You cherish the memories of someone who has died and these bring you comfort.

- If you have an illness, you adapt the best you can and make the most of your capabilities.

For most people you can see that anxiety often comes about because of change, but that anxiety leads to new actions. You find a way of overcoming anxiety. You can even find that life turns out better because of this.

However, occasionally we all get stuck for a while. If a new partner does not prove any better than the last, or if the new job is terrible, or your illness makes you feel much worse than you thought, things can indeed become very bleak for a while. Generally, however, people keep on going, trying new things. Or they simply accept the situation, try not to get down about things they cannot control, and turn to some other aspect of their life that gives them pleasure.

People often get stuck with anxiety when a number of events all happen very close to each other. Or if you try to overcome a problem and do not succeed, your anxiety can increase:

- You can feel overwhelmed.

'You find a way of overcoming anxiety. You can even find that life turns out better because of this.'

- You can get fearful.

- You don't want even more change so you avoid anything that could make things worse.

- You avoid things.

- You seek some solace and reassurance from those around you, but it makes things no better.

- You start to have depressive thoughts.

- You see danger lurking.

- You feel like a loser.

- You doubt yourself.

- You hate your life.

'People who suffer from anxiety get stuck with patterns of thinking that make things worse.'

People who suffer from anxiety get stuck with patterns of thinking that make things worse. These negative thoughts go hand in hand with bad feelings, feelings of anxiety and gloom.

By learning to understand your own anxiety, by taking a good look at yourself, you are taking the first step to getting rid of that anxiety and living a normal life.

Summing Up

Before you can start to overcome your anxiety problems you first have to take a good look at your own anxiety. You need to be able to describe exactly what your problems are. You need to know how it feels when you are anxious and how your thoughts go along with these feelings. Then you need to reflect on what your anxiety makes you do, how you behave, how your anxiety makes you interact with others. You might be able to see how your anxiety started and that is interesting, but it does not matter if you cannot find a trigger. You must appreciate that major change brings about anxiety. You can then learn to accommodate to this change. By taking a close and detailed look at your own pattern of anxiety you can start to spot ways to improve things for the better.

Chapter Four

Anxiety Timeline

You are about to learn to become your own therapist. Before you can tackle your anxiety it will be very helpful if, at this point, you can get a little notebook, and start to put your reflections on paper.

This will serve a number of purposes.

■ Firstly, it will help you to remember key points in your personal plan of action.

■ Secondly, it will help you think about your anxiety as a separate thing from the essential you, your mind, your body, your true self. Your anxiety is something that you can write about, put outside of yourself and into a notebook.

Therefore, by starting to write about your anxiety, you are learning to control it by externalising it. You start to look at your anxiety as something separate from the real you. It is just another problem that you can look at and learn to deal with. It will no longer consume you.

'Anxiety is just another problem that you can look at and learn to deal with.'

Anxiety: beginning, middle, end

By now you will have started to really think about your anxiety and you will have thought about a timeline:

■ Beginning – the cause of your anxiety.

■ Middle – what the anxiety is like for you.

■ End – how you try to control the anxiety when it comes.

We can look a little more closely at each of these in turn.

Beginning – the cause of your anxiety

If you have had anxiety for a long time, you might not be able to pinpoint an exact cause, but if you can, write it down.

If you really have no idea what started your anxiety in the first place, think about your experience of anxiety now.

- What will start the anxious thoughts, behaviours and feelings?

- What might you be doing at the time they start?

- What time of day does anxiety strike?

- Is it associated with a certain place, person, a certain thought?

Try to think deeply about these four aspects. Try to take as objective a view as you can.

Many people find, when they take a close look at themselves, that they can paint a very real picture of their problem. Here are some examples:

- For Mary, her main anxiety is fear of going outdoors. The problem began when she lost her husband and she felt isolated, fearful and vulnerable. That started it all off, but now the feelings of anxiety start if she even thinks about the possibility of going outdoors. If anyone suggests going out, a family meal, a holiday, the feelings of anxiety start.

- For Ben, he is anxious at work. He feels that his manager is getting at him. The anxiety starts as soon as he wakes up in the morning and he knows it is a work day. Going into work makes the anxiety increase even more. Opening up his emails sees another sudden surge of worry. Another cause of the anxiety feeling comes at the end of the day, just sitting at home his thoughts make him anxious as he goes over in his mind some of the things that happened in work that day.

- For Martha, her anxiety is about the children. Her feelings of responsibility started when she married. She was happy at first and is happy now really, but she worries something bad is going to happen. So her anxiety starts as she sees the children go out. 'Will they be alright, manage the roads, and not get into any accidents?' Thoughts about her children immediately provoke an anxiety response. 'Will they be safe outdoors? Indeed, will they be safe indoors? Are things clean enough? Is the house safe?'

Think about what causes your anxiety. Write it down because you will want to return to it as you reflect on your situation.

Middle – what the anxiety is like for you

You say you feel anxious but what do you mean? In the previous chapters I have described some of the common symptoms of anxiety but they might not all apply to you. Focus on your own personal experiences and try to describe in detail what your anxiety reaction is. What is often helpful is to divide up your anxiety experience into three different headings:

- Mind – the thoughts in your head.
- Body – internal sensations and feelings of emotion.
- Behaviour – ways you act when anxious.

Mind – the thoughts in your head

When you feel anxiety what are your specific thoughts? Write down exactly what goes through your head, the words as you speak them to yourself.

To begin this you will probably be trying to recall your thoughts so what you write may not be entirely accurate. However, think back to an anxiety-provoking situation and try to recall words. You may not be able to form the thoughts into complete sentences but that really does not matter. Here are some examples of thoughts that go along with anxiety:

- 'They might be killed.'
- 'I am going to die.'
- 'I am not good enough.'
- 'I can't cope.'
- 'I am going to lose my job.'

- 'People will laugh at me.'

- 'I am going to let everyone down.'

- 'This is unsafe.'

- 'I think I am really ill.'

- 'This is cancer.'

- 'I can't get my breath.'

- 'I hate my life.'

- 'I am useless.'

- 'I always fail.'

- 'I can't do this.'

- 'I am stupid.'

- 'They won't love me anymore.'

- 'I am going to ruin everyone else's good time if I can't do this.'

- 'I am not as good as the others.'

- 'I am out of control.'

- 'I am such a loser.'

These are all typical examples of thoughts that accompany a feeling of anxiety, the actual words spoken in the head. Just look through this list. Imagine someone thinking these kinds of things on a daily basis, just uttering the words to themselves. How is it going to make them feel? They are going to worry. The words themselves are likely to lead to feelings of anxiety and will keep the anxiety going day to day. The words themselves can easily lead to low self-esteem, lack of confidence and depression to accompany the anxiety.

As well as thinking about, and trying to remember and write down your thoughts, I want you to have your notebook by you for a day and, as the anxious thoughts arise, write them down as they happen.

If you have different types of anxious thoughts in different situations use a number of headings to make your recordings. Here is an example for work anxiety, the way Ben might think:

At work Ben thinks:

- 'Another email off him, oh no!'
- 'I am never going to make this deadline.'
- 'They have all gone out to lunch without me.'
- 'They are talking behind my back.'

But once at home, Ben's anxiety makes him think:

- 'Another useless day.'
- 'I am going to lose my job.'
- 'Why am I such a failure in life?'
- 'My family will suffer.'

Here is an example of the thoughts that Mary might have, the anxious words that run through her brain that are related to her fear of going outdoors:

- 'Another day stuck inside, I am useless.'
- 'My daughter so wants me to come on holiday but I can't.'
- 'I will be letting them all down by not going.'
- 'I can't go, I will panic too much.'
- 'I will faint, I could fall, I could break a bone.'
- 'My heart will be beating so fast I will die.'

Finally, here is an example of the thoughts Martha has when she thinks about her children:

- 'They will not remember to look before crossing the road.'
- 'The oldest one keeps bad company.'
- 'What if they get ill?'
- 'It is my duty to make sure they eat right and everything is spotless.'
- 'I worry about additives in their food.'
- 'What if one of them has an asthma attack and dies?'

■ 'I had better make sure I check the gas is properly off or else someone could die.'

Body – internal sensations and feelings of emotion

We have seen that the body reacts in very particular ways as a result of anxiety. Remind yourself of some of the typical physical reactions that accompany anxious thoughts and behaviours by looking back at the beginning of chapter 2.

Try to separate out your thoughts that go with anxiety from the feelings within your body. What do you feel when you are anxious?

Different people tend to focus on different internal sensations. For example:

■ It might be that mostly you feel dizzy or lightheaded.

■ Or do you feel physically sick?

■ Or is the main thing a sensation of your heart pounding?

■ Do you sweat a lot?

■ Do you tense up?

■ Get headaches?

■ Get a dry mouth and find it difficult to talk?

■ Do you get the urge to go to the toilet?

■ Do you find you can't concentrate?

'Try to separate out your thoughts that go with anxiety from the feelings within your body.'

Write a list of the things that you feel, the internal sensations you experience that you associate with your anxiety.

Try to create as full a description as you can and then think about what happens first. Do you feel dizzy then sick? Is there any sequence at all or do you have these feelings all together?

Maybe you get your anxiety reactions more severely at some times rather than others.

■ How does your body feel when you are just a little or moderately anxious?

■ And how does it feel when you are as anxious as can be?

Reflect on what makes you react in the way you do. Is there a particular cause that will bring on a strong sensation of anxiety? What brings on slight anxiety?

The purpose of this exercise is for you to learn to reflect on your own body, to learn the situations that make you respond with the internal reactions that you associate with feelings of anxiety.

Almost certainly you will not look at your body's reaction in a purely descriptive way. You will attach little labels to those internal feelings, and those will most likely be emotional labels.

▓ So, along with the fast heartbeat, your emotion may be one of fear or dread.

▓ Your physiological responses you may label as anger in some situations.

▓ You may say your tense muscles are a sign of stress.

Such emotional labels are things that people typically use when they suffer from anxiety. What emotions do you associate with your anxiety?

Behaviour – ways you act when anxious

When you feel anxious how do you act? What are the observable behaviours that go along with your feelings and thoughts about anxiety? There are so many things that people do when they feel anxious that it is difficult to make a typical list. Undoubtedly, you will have built up your own particular repertoire or set of actions that accompany your anxiety and it is important for you to reflect on these and write them down.

Here is an example of the types of actions that Martha takes when she feels anxious about her children:

▓ She phones or texts them to see if they are alright.

▓ She does a lot of cleaning around the house.

▓ She talks to her sister about her worries, phones her most days in fact.

▓ She eats a lot as that is very comforting.

Now, none of these things is that unusual, but Martha has found that she is spending too long cleaning and checking things are right. Her children say she texts too much, her phone bill is enormous, and she is getting upset as her clothes are now too tight because of her comfort eating. In brief, her actions are not working in the long term to reduce her anxiety. It is still there but she is now short of money and overweight.

What does Ben do when he is anxious about work? Well, he cannot avoid going in, but here are some of the actions that go along with his anxiety:

- He tries to drum up support for himself by talking to other colleagues about his boss behind his back.
- He fires off emails which are heavily critical of his employers.
- He stops for a few drinks on the way home and then has a few more when at home, just to try to calm himself down.
- He is bad-tempered with his family.

You can see that some of these actions are not really related to anxiety in a direct way. Rather, Ben has started to change his habits, his health has started to deteriorate. As well as this, he has started to change his interactions with others. His colleagues wonder what is up with him. His family is beginning to question what has happened to make him so distant and bad-tempered.

But what does Mary do to help her cope with her fear of going outdoors? Well, she decides that her action will be to spend a lot of time indoors, to avoid going out as much as possible. Her behaviour, directly associated with her anxiety is this:

- She sits and watches television a great deal.
- She has started buying puzzle books to pass the time.
- She likes to browse the web on the computer.

With all of these things she feels safe. However, she knows that time is passing her by and deep down she knows she is not enjoying the life she thought she would be leading. Therefore, sometimes, her actions show her disappointment:

- She asks a friend to come round and sit with her.
- When her daughter visits she asks her to take her to the GP; perhaps she could get some medication to help her feel a bit braver, more adventurous.

■ She cuts down on her spending; she cannot get out and get a job and so she has less money.

End – how you try to control the anxiety when it comes

You will find that you behave in certain ways because you experience anxiety. You may well find that many of your actions will be habits that you have picked up to try to control your anxiety in some way.

In the examples here you can see that, for Martha, Ben and Mary, many of their anxiety-related behaviours have developed as a means to control anxiety.

Their actions work short term, but long term the anxiety remains. In fact some of the short-term actions are detrimental to health. Drinking too much or eating too much on a daily basis is going to compound the anxiety problem.

Reflect on each action/behaviour you have written down related to your personal anxiety:

■ Does that action happen almost automatically?

■ Can you keep from doing the action?

■ To what extent does it help you control your anxiety?

■ How long before the anxiety comes back?

■ Why does it not make the anxiety go away long term?

Anxiety can be a truly horrible sensation and it is therefore predictable that you try to control it. You develop little habits or start to use people for help or to give you much needed reassurance. Or you avoid the thing that makes you anxious. What are the ways that you try to control your anxiety?

We have talked about mind (your thoughts), body (your internal reactions and emotions) and your behaviours (your actions). What do you do to 'put yourself right' when you experience anxiety? Write your reflections now in your notebook. If other things come to mind as you progress through this book you can always revisit your list and add to it.

Summing Up

Now is the start of your own self-analysis. It is ideal to get a notebook and to write down essential points about your personal experience of anxiety. Firstly, you consider the cause of your anxiety. That means what caused it in the first place, but also what causes anxiety day to day. Secondly, you must think about the actual anxiety itself. There are different strands to this and it is useful to consider your thoughts, your bodily sensations and emotions, and your behaviour, as separate things. By breaking down your understanding of your anxiety into different components you are starting to divide up your anxiety into more manageable pieces.

'Consider your thoughts, your bodily sensations and emotions, and your behaviours as separate things; start to divide up your anxiety into more manageable pieces.'

Chapter Five

Anxiety Circle

You have seen that anxiety can be understood as a timeline. Anxiety starts with a cause, then it exists as an entity which affects your mind, your body, and your behaviour. You feel anxiety and it is unpleasant. Therefore, at the end of the timeline you act to try to reduce your anxiety.

So, when you experience anxiety it is uncomfortable for you. You might behave in a certain way to reduce the anxiety, or avoid things, or chat to someone. There are any number of things you can do and you will have listed your coping mechanisms as you were shown at the end of the last chapter.

Now, if your coping methods worked well, the anxiety would go away and stay away. The timeline would finish there and you would be happy.

For some people this is how it works for much of the time; a small anxiety comes along, discomfort is felt. The person puzzles about how to cope, comes up with a workable solution, acts on it, and normal functioning is restored. The anxiety timeline has started and finished.

When your coping mechanisms do not work

Anxiety sometimes stays with you. That can be for a number of reasons:

- Sometimes the problem that is causing the anxiety is too big to solve in one go.

- Or the problem may be one that it is going to take a long time to put right.

- It could be that there is no obvious cause to the anxiety and no obvious solution.

- Maybe you cannot relax enough to see that your anxiety will fade away over time simply by leaving it there and doing nothing.

If you still have anxiety despite the things you do to try to overcome it, you might want to reflect on how useful your coping mechanisms are. Go through your list and consider how effective your actions are, the things you do to try to cope with anxiety. For each of your examples rate how effective it is, both in the short term and in the long term. Make your rating out of 10. To give you some help with this let us first look at the actions that Martha, Ben and Mary take in order to reduce their anxiety.

Martha

Here is the example for Martha, who is anxious about her children. We saw in the previous chapter that she behaves in these ways when she worries about them:

- She phones or texts them to see if they are alright.
- She does a lot of cleaning around the house.
- She talks to her sister about her worries, phones her most days in fact.
- She eats a lot as that is very comforting.

When Martha looks at these behaviours she finds that they all work very well to reduce her anxiety. They work short term and that is exactly why she keeps on doing them day after day.

- If her anxiety is high, she rates her usual daily high level as 8/10, then talking to her sister will reduce it to about 3/10.
- Cleaning will reduce it to 2/10, but if she works really hard all day then it can reduce to 1/10, hardly any anxiety at all.
- She finds that eating is pretty good for anxiety, a nice cake and cup of tea will see an immediate reduction of her anxiety to about 3/10.
- Texting can reduce her anxiety but only if that child texts back. If she does not receive a return text then her anxiety can soar right up to a full 10/10.

The thing to notice here, the thing that strikes Martha as she looks at her ratings, is that although her actions bring some relief it does not last long. An hour or less and she begins her obsessive worrying again.

'If you still have anxiety despite the things you do to try to overcome it, you might want to reflect on how useful your coping mechanisms are.'

The anxiety circles round, back to the start. She starts to feel anxious, she has her feelings of dread and all her physiological signs of worry are there again. Her anxious thoughts come right back. And so she sits and eats, or phones, or texts, or cleans again.

Ben

When Ben is anxious here are some of the things he does to try to cope, as we saw in the last chapter:

- He tries to drum up support for himself by talking to other colleagues about his boss behind his back.

- He fires off emails which are heavily critical of his employers.

- He stops for a few drinks on the way home and then has a few more when at home, just to try to calm himself down.

- He is bad-tempered with his family.

Ben thinks about how effective these things are. These are things he does every work day so he is pretty sure they are helping. However, when he tries to rate how effective his coping strategies are he finds things are less clear than he thought.

- Although he gets immediate relief from talking to work colleagues, his anxiety falls from 9/10 to around 2/10, he has found that it all depends on who he confides in. Recently, a person that he thought of as a friend has looked a bit fed up when Ben talks to him. He worries that his friend is starting to think of him as a loser.

- Although Ben has been in the habit of sending emails to friends just to let off steam (a good anxiety reduction from 9/10 down to 5/10) he is horrified to find that one of these has been forwarded on through the company. What if the boss gets to see what he has written?

- Ben has found that drinking has a great and profound relaxing effect, it can reduce his anxiety levels from 9/10 right down to 0/10. However, that is only for the first few drinks. By the end of the night, if he has been drinking steadily through the evening, he can start to feel depressed and his anxiety rises again unless he drinks himself almost into a coma.

- Ben has to bite his tongue during the day in work, appear polite in front of managers. He finds that he then retaliates at home by trying to take control of the children or saying uncomplimentary things to his wife. By trying to be 'the boss of his own home' he finds that reduces his anxiety a bit, down to 4/10, because he feels more in control.

Looking at this picture Ben realises two things:

- Firstly, despite the relief that his actions bring him, the basic problem stays the same. He is anxious about his work and that anxiety returns each morning. He hates his job.

- Secondly, he sees that he has become a different sort of person because of the ways he was chosen to deal with his anxiety. He fears he is becoming an alcoholic. He certainly has put on weight because of his drinking. He hates the way he looks. Also he used to be something of a family man, still loves his wife and kids, but he feels he is distancing himself from them. If his wife divorces him that would just be the end.

Mary

Mary copes with her agoraphobia in a number of ways. She tries to make the most of her time at home which she decides is a positive thing. As we saw in the last chapter:

- She sits and watches television a great deal.
- She has started buying puzzle books to pass the time.
- She likes to browse the web on the computer.

When she is doing these things she finds she is not anxious at all. She bubbles along with an anxiety level of zero, at the very maximum 1/10.

So, from a certain perspective Mary should be a happy woman. Indeed some people stay at home for long periods of time and are quite content to be that way. However, that is a very small percentage of the population. That does not apply to Mary.

By not going out, Mary realises that she is not achieving her true potential for happiness. She would like to do the simple things, like going shopping by herself. She knows she would get a tremendous feeling of personal achievement and joy if only she could go on holiday with her daughter and grandchildren. She also would quite like a job, maybe something part time, to earn a bit more money.

Therefore, for most of her day, Mary has a deep-rooted feeling of inadequacy, of a life not quite lived as it should be.

However, if she even thinks seriously about going outside she feels her anxiety soar. It goes from 1/10 to 9/10. If she even walks to the front gate to take out the rubbish bin the anxiety is 9/10 too, she feels her heart pounding, she feels faint. The only way she can control her anxiety is to stay in, keep the level low.

If she absolutely has to go out, to the GP or dentist, she has to have someone with her. Even then the anxiety is as high as 8/10 or 9/10.

Your anxiety circle

You should now be ready to think about your circle of anxiety.

- Rate each thing you do to try to cope so you can see how effective it is at reducing anxiety.

- Now consider how long your anxiety stays away for each of your anxiety-reducing actions.

- What are the negative effects of each thing you do? Are your actions backfiring on you?

- Of the actions you take, are there any you could drop out of your repertoire?

Which will require more work to get rid of them? What anxiety-related behaviour can be dropped from the list?

Think about your list and reflect on what your actions say about you. Is there anything that you currently do that you could just stop? In the example with Ben, one of the easiest things he could do is simply stop sending emails where he is talking about people. He knows this is just a small thing, but it might save him more trouble in the long term.

Perhaps the next thing he might tackle is to not complain about his boss so much to so many people. Having one close person to confide in is helpful, but perhaps he should try to keep it at that.

The drinking problem might take longer to solve, but at least he will feel he is making a start if he can cut down a little bit. And anyway, deep down he knows his best solution to his anxiety is to quietly stick with the job until he can find himself another one.

'Think about your list and reflect on what your actions say about you. Is there anything that you currently do that you could just stop?'

With Martha, always worrying about her children, once she looks at her list she realises that texting and phoning them is only making her worse because she worries more if she does not get an immediate reply. Therefore, that behaviour can be the first to go.

With Mary, she realises that she has been burying her head in the sand by avoiding going out. She starts to see that unless she takes positive steps she will be at home by herself for the rest of her days.

You need to closely look at your own anxiety circle. You will find that your anxiety is being maintained by what you are doing:

- Your thoughts will be negative. You allow yourself to think catastrophic things and you put yourself down 'I cannot cope', 'This is dangerous', 'The worst will happen unless I carry on the way I have been doing'.

- Your body will react to your thoughts and you will have at least some of the physical symptoms of anxiety. Those symptoms – pounding heart, breathlessness, giddiness – will circle round and feed into your mind to create more negative thoughts.

- Your actions, your very behaviour that you use to cope with your anxiety, will make you worse. You might avoid the feared situation but your anxiety stays. The things you do to help with your anxiety are so short term and ineffective that the anxiety returns again and again.

In the next few chapters you will see that if you break your goals down into small manageable steps they add up to helping you solve your problems. You have to learn to look at and manage your thoughts, your body, and your behaviour.

Summing Up

In this chapter we have looked in more detail at coping mechanisms, the actions that people take to try to overcome their anxiety. Most of these behaviours work, but sadly they only work short term. People come to depend on them for immediate relief and find it difficult to stop. One way to overcome these maladaptive behaviour patterns is to take a close look at them. Rate how much they reduce anxiety. But then consider how long the anxiety stays away. Those behaviour patterns that are not so useful can be dropped first. To break the anxiety circle will take time and it will be necessary to take a separate look at how to deal with thoughts, the body's physiological reactions to stress and the behaviours that only bring short-term relief.

'To break the anxiety circle will take time.'

Chapter Six

Control Your Body

Nowhere to run and nowhere to hide

We have seen that anxiety can have a variety of physiological effects. Many of these happen automatically. When your heart pounds or you feel dizzy or sick, or experience any of the physical symptoms associated with anxiety; they are usually a pretty immediate reaction to threat. You have an anxiety-related thought or you see a situation that you perceive as threatening and your body responds.

This is great if the pumping adrenalin gives you the impetus to flee from danger. But if the danger is in your mind then there is nowhere to run, nowhere to hide. You are left with a body in a state of high alert, high anxiety, and for no good reason. You could run like the wind, but running will not help.

Here is the thing, if you actually do nothing, if you stop using your ineffective coping mechanisms, your high arousal levels will fall by themselves. Your body simply cannot maintain that ultra high level of arousal that happens when you perceive danger. As the minutes tick on you will see that the worst has not happened. The message to the body is that nothing bad has happened this minute, nothing bad has happened the next minute, and so on. The body realises that it does not need to be ready to act, to run away, to fight a foe. Tension gradually dissipates and you return to a normal resting level.

The level of arousal, of high anxiety, of panic, can be felt just as keenly by a person with agoraphobia going outside as a person being genuinely threatened, for example, in a violent attack and in real danger.

'We have seen that anxiety can have a variety of physiological effects. Many of these happen automatically.'

The 'just leave it alone' technique

Some therapists take the view that you should learn to ignore the body's signals of anxiety and you will quickly learn that your body will bring itself down to a normal level of functioning. It will do this all by itself in a relatively short period of time.

This is indeed true. If you feel you want to try this then do so. If you are slightly scared to do it you might want to have someone with you for the first couple of occasions you try it. Sit quietly and feel the fear fade as you calmly breathe.

'When you feel high anxiety you will unconsciously start to breathe in a different way. You will breathe quite quickly and shallowly, using the top part of your lungs.'

If you feel complete panic, a complete state of high anxiety, try if you possibly can to look objectively at yourself. Yes indeed your anxiety is at that full 10 out of 10 level. Now stop. Simply stop and do nothing. Wait for a minute, two if you can. How high is the level now? Sit down if there is something you can sit on. Keep as still as you can. Try to relax. How high is your anxiety level now?

You should find as the minutes tick on that your anxiety level reduces minute by minute, all by itself. Give yourself 10 to 15 minutes to feel the full effect.

Learn to breathe in the right way

However, most people trying to control anxiety find it rather difficult to simply ignore their anxiety reaction. If this applies to you then you will be pleased to learn that there are positive things that you can do to help you control your anxiety response. You can act in such a way that you can learn to control your physiological responses.

If you behave in certain ways, think in certain ways, you can reduce a raised heartbeat, stop the panic, you can feel in control and, indeed, be in control.

When you feel high anxiety, you will unconsciously start to breathe in a different way. You will breathe quite quickly and shallowly, using the top part of your lungs. Counteract this:

- If you want to feel calm, breathe slowly and regularly from the bottom of your lungs.

- Start with just a few calming breaths.

- Say to yourself 'one – two – three – in' as you breathe in. Imagine as you breathe in that you are pulling all your anxiety feelings up out of your body into your mouth.

- Then say to yourself 'one – two – three – out' as you push your breath out of your mouth.

- As you breathe out, imagine your anxiety going out of your mouth. Push it out of your body. Push out absolutely all the way, as far as you can. Your body will then react by making the next breath inwards a really deep and effective one.

It is important to do this calmly and slowly. There is no point breathing deeply and quickly for minutes on end as you will end up with too much oxygen in your system and that in itself will make you feel lightheaded, the opposite of what you are trying to achieve. No, just a few deep, slow, calm breaths, counting the air in and counting the air out, pushing out the anxiety in your mind along with the air from your lungs. That is all that is needed. Take between three and five deep breaths when you really feel anxious and this will automatically make you feel calmer.

If you are worried about how it might make you feel, start by practising this exercise in bed. Do it before you go to sleep.

It seems almost childishly simple to breathe away your problems and yet it really can be a big factor in learning to control your body. And the beauty of it is that anyone can do it, anytime, anywhere.

Mental imagery and breathing

When you breathe out your anxiety you can imagine it as a black fog in your body that you are pulling up and out. Imagine your body being emptied of the blackness with every breath. When you have made a few deep breaths and you are just breathing slowly, calmly, carry on visualising the black turning to grey as it leaves your body. Finally, imagine that the anxiety is gone and the out-breath is just clear.

Next, imagine that you want to fill your body and mind with peace and positivity. Imagine the air coming into your body is now a misty gold colour, the colour of sunny happiness. Imagine with each breath that it is filling your body from your toes, up the legs, into the main body, arms, neck and head. Then see yourself as having a golden glow all over.

Although you might want to practise this at home and perhaps do it in bed at night or lying on the couch, this really is a very easy technique that you can use whenever you are in an anxiety-provoking situation.

If you recognise that you are anxious, you can take two or three deep breaths and quickly empty your body of the black anxiety. Then breathe calmly and deeply a few times and imagine the gold colour coming into you, bringing peace and making you confident.

Relax your muscles

'A relaxed body will lead to a relaxed mind.'

There are some muscles in your body that are involuntary, that you will not just be able to relax. However, in terms of the anxiety response, you can learn to control the major muscle groups where anxiety is manifested as tension.

- A relaxed body will lead to a relaxed mind.
- A relaxed mind will lead to a relaxed body.

As you can see the anxiety response can circle round in lots of ways. You have to learn where to step in and try to take control of what is happening in the way that is right for you.

It is all well and good to say 'relax' but to do that immediately, on command, is very difficult. It is a sign of the times we live in that most of us do not know what a relaxed body truly feels like.

You can learn to relax by starting out, by yourself, in the comfort of your own bed. If you haven't the time to do this during the day, do it at night before you go to sleep. Lie flat and start with your breathing exercises, counting in slowly and then counting out slowly, pushing all the way out, imagining your anxiety leaving your body with your breath.

Then you are ready to start. Basically, you will find it easier to recognise what a relaxed muscle feels like if you start by deliberately tensing it. You will have to work systematically around your body first tensing then relaxing your muscles.

- Each time you tense a muscle try to keep it tense, contracted tight, to a count of 8 to 10 seconds. Then let go and count to 30 and concentrate your thoughts on that muscle as it relaxes.

- Then repeat this for the same muscle group, contracting as hard as you can for 8 to 10 seconds, then relaxing for 30 seconds, counting as you go.

Using this 'tense then relax' technique you can slowly work round the body, tensing and relaxing each muscle group twice. I would suggest that you work from the toes upwards to your head. Try to use the same routine all the time so it becomes automatic. Try a week of doing this every time you go to bed. Here is the order in which to tense then relax each muscle group, remembering to do each muscle group twice:

- Left leg – foot (bending your toes back or forward) and calf muscle.

- Left thigh and buttock.

- Right leg: foot (bending toes as before) and calf muscle.

- Right thigh and buttock.

- Stomach muscles.

- Shoulders – raise and scrunch up to your ears.

- Shoulders – pull them right back against the bed (if you like you can tense your stomach muscles again too if that helps you).

- Left arm – clench your fist and try to tense your whole arm.

- Right arm – again, clench your fist and try to tense your whole arm.

- Face – scrunch up your face, then open your eyes and mouth wide and hold that position, almost in a silent scream.

Remember, for each of these you tense for 8-10 seconds, then you let go counting for 30. As you let go really focus on the muscle group you have just tensed. Feel the muscle relaxing.

When you are completely relaxed, imagine that your body is heavy and feel the warmth of your muscles. Concentrate on that feeling, imagining your body getting heavier and warmer as the seconds tick away.

Before you get up, or before you fall asleep, picture the most beautiful scene that you can. What would be your ideal place? Then imagine yourself there, feeling great, and with not a care in the world.

If you have practised the full relaxation procedure each day for a few days or weeks, you can shorten the process if you wish. Maybe just tense and relax each muscle group once rather than twice. Or, if you do not have much time, lie down and tense your whole body as much as you can for about 10 seconds, then feel it relax as you count to 30. Feel your body warm and heavy, breathe out your anxiety.

'When you are completely relaxed, imagine that your body is heavy and feel the warmth of your muscles.'

If you want to play soothing music through this whole process, that is an added extra that you can choose. You will start to associate the feeling of relaxation with the sound of the music. That can be useful if you want to put the track on an mp3 player that you can then listen to any time you start to feel anxious. Just hearing it will remind you to be calm and relaxed.

Taking it further

You will probably want to start by practising this alone, in your bed, all by yourself in the darkness!

Over a couple of weeks you will start to appreciate what tension feels like and what relaxation feels like.

When you are going about your normal, everyday activities, pause to stop occasionally and think how your body is feeling.

- Are you tense, and if so, where?
- People very commonly have tense shoulders, their bodies hunched over a computer or desk.

What are the times and places where you tense up? Start to apply your relaxation techniques in everyday situations. Obviously you will have to do this slightly differently from when you are in the privacy of your own bedroom. You may not be able to tense your muscles prior to relaxation. But you can:

- Slowly and deeply breathe in and out a few times, counting the breath in and breathing your anxiety out.

- You can drop your shoulders lower, relaxing them with each breath.

- You can relax your facial muscles. Stop frowning, relax the muscles around your eyes, ease off the tension in the muscles around your mouth.

- Move your shoulders around a little. Have a stretch, then relax some more.

Try to get to that stage where you recognise the signs of stress, worry, anxiety, as they start. Apply your strategies to counteract these feelings.

Using colour with the muscle-relaxation technique

We have already seen that you can imagine anxiety as blackness that you breathe out of your body, and then you fill your body with golden peaceful air.

What you can do with the relaxation technique is imagine this:

- When you tense your muscles, imagine them filling with black colour. As you tense harder and longer the colour should go from grey to dark grey to black.

- Then, as you let go of the tension, imagine the colour draining away as the muscle relaxes, fading to grey then white. Finally the white colour should start to go to a calming golden glow that infuses the muscles.

The importance of appearances

Imagine a confident person, one you know personally or someone from the television or film. How do they stand? How do they sit? How do they walk? When they speak, what is the tone of their voice?

If you start to behave as if you have no anxiety, if you behave as a confident person, you will start to feel confident. If you have high self-esteem, if you believe in your own abilities, this will help you to conquer anxiety.

'If you behave as a confident person, you will start to feel confident. If you have high self-esteem, if you believe in your own abilities, this will help you to conquer anxiety.'

Think about the way you behave when you are anxious. Picture in your mind what your body is like.

- Are your shoulders hunched or is your back nice and straight?
- Do you timidly walk along or stride out confidently?
- Do you sound worried when you speak or do you sound quietly assured?

Think consciously about these aspects of yourself and deliberately practise your confident behaviour.

Change your verbal behaviour

When you are anxious, what do you say, what sort of things do you chat about with others? If you talk a great deal about yourself and your anxiety problem, that topic may just expand and fill your mind and fill your life. Others may start to view you as someone who finds it hard to cope.

If you have an anxiety issue that has been with you for weeks, months, even years, how much has talking about it really helped? Even if you just get short-term relief from talking or seeking reassurance, if the anxiety problem remains with you then you have been using a poor strategy to deal with it. In fact, repeatedly seeking reassurance will actually make the anxiety more likely to linger with you long term. Deliberately monitor how much you talk about your anxiety. Write it down for a single day or week:

- Notice how many minutes you talk for, how long the conversation goes on.
- Notice who it is that you talk to about your anxiety.

Now deliberately, the following week, try not to talk about your anxiety at all. See how long you can keep this up for. Your anxiety might rise slightly at first, so remember your breathing techniques and the mental imagery that goes with it, the colours changing from black to gold as your muscles relax and your mind goes calm.

If you find you can only go a short time without talking about your anxieties, note that time and then try again not to talk about it. Try to beat your record. Keep on this way until talking about your anxiety, seeking reassurance, is a thing of the past.

Emphasise the positive

If you are trying to change, to get rid of behaviour associated with anxiety, think about what you are going to replace the negative behaviour with.

- What can you do that makes you happy?

- What can you talk about that is interesting and positive?

- Can you get more interested in other people's lives? Sometimes it is good to listen and not talk.

- Are there new hobbies you could try?

- What interests could you really immerse yourself in?

- How about planning a holiday?

You may need to make changes in your life if you are going to keep anxiety at bay. Some changes can be easier than others. However, even if some problems are going to take a while to fix, you can still practise relaxation, stay calm, appear confident. How you behave affects your mood and the way you think.

Summing Up

Your body reacts to anxiety in specific ways. Without realising it, you breathe differently and tense your muscles when you are worried. Anxiety will slowly ebb away if you do not react to it. However, what can be helpful is if you learn to consciously relax your body. If you take a few deep breaths and learn how to relax your muscles this will help reduce anxiety. Mental imagery is useful too. You can imagine black to be tension and represent your anxiety. As you breathe out you expel the blackness, get rid of the tension. As you relax you then fill the space within you with a calm golden glow. If you change your posture and tone of voice to reflect confidence then you change the way you view yourself and the way that others see you. You will start to see yourself as a confident person, not an anxious person. If you talk about your anxiety, if you give it space, then it will start to consume you. Do not seek reassurance but think about filling your life with new, more positive behaviours.

'Do not seek reassurance but think about filling your life with new, more positive behaviours.'

Chapter Seven

Time for Action

Avoidance

We have seen that one of the most common strategies that people use to cope with anxiety is to avoid the thing that makes then anxious. In the short term that brings people immediate relief; their fear goes. Therefore, it is not surprising that people use avoidance as a method of coping with anxiety.

It is perfectly normal to avoid things that bring on unpleasant feelings. We all do it. Much of the time it has no great effect on our lives. For example:

- You might avoid a food you don't like the taste of.

- You might not bother talking to someone you dislike.

- You choose to not watch certain TV programmes because you don't like them.

So you express a preference. You try to keep happy by doing what you like and avoiding the things you don't like.

Where this system can go wrong is when you want to do something or have something, but the process of getting to the end point makes you anxious. You learn to fear.

- You want to go on holiday but you are frightened of travelling.

- You want to go shopping but you are afraid to go out alone.

- You want to make friends and socialise but you fear making a fool of yourself.

'It is perfectly normal to avoid things that bring on unpleasant feelings. We all do it. Much of the time it has no great effect on our lives.'

Or you might want to feel more competent, more in control of yourself, but you have a fear or phobia that bothers you. You might function day to day perfectly well, but if you see a spider you become a wreck. Phobias can quickly build and by avoiding the feared response you are unlikely to get over it.

When you become anxious or feel fear, you cope by running away or avoiding. You don't give yourself the opportunity to realise that the fear response will ebb away. It will go even though you are still in the presence of the feared thing.

- Avoidance is not the way to overcome anxiety.

- You have to face the thing you fear if you want to overcome anxiety.

- Fear will burn itself out within a very short time if you just allow it to.

This makes sense if you think about it. If you are socially anxious but avoid groups of people, you will never learn to mingle and chat. If you are frightened of going outdoors, you will not lose that anxiety if you stay at home. If you are scared of spiders, you have to learn to face them and cope with them if you want that anxiety to go. If you are anxious about making a speech at a big event, don't avoid thinking about it; you have to practise it if you want to do well. If you are anxious about exams, don't avoid revision. If you are going to a job interview, don't avoid thinking about it but practise what you might say.

You can see that avoidance can make things very much worse. The most anxious people are nearly always those who use avoidance as their main way of coping.

You therefore have to deliberately expose yourself to the thing you fear.

Exposure

Deliberately exposing yourself to your fear is a major part of overcoming anxiety. However, the very idea of doing that might be a stimulus for your anxiety to start. Well-meaning friends might inadvertently make it worse by forcing you to act, doing too much too soon. You might even have scared yourself by plunging yourself into a situation that was so frightening that it made matters worse.

It is best to take a systematic approach. You need to make a stepped plan to achieve your goal.

'Deliberately exposing yourself to your fear is a major part of overcoming anxiety. However, the very idea of doing that might be a stimulus for your anxiety to start.'

Let us think back to Mary who we talked about in chapters 4 and 5. You will remember that her anxiety is related to agoraphobia. She is anxious about going out alone. She is quite happy when at home, but deep down she knows she is not living life to the full. She wants to be able to go to the shops by herself. She would love to go on holiday with her daughter and the grandchildren. She would like a little part-time job that would mean leaving the house.

To be able to do any of these things she needs to overcome her fear of going outside by herself.

She thinks about what her first main goal might be. It should be something that she can write down, something concrete and attainable. It is no good to just write that she wants to feel less anxious. It has to be objective.

Therefore, she decides that her goal will be to walk to the nearest shops, about 10 minutes away, to buy her favourite magazine, and walk back home with it. That is her aim. She uses a notebook to write down a series of mini goals, small steps or stages that will see her to goal.

This describes her mini goals and her progress with each of them:

- Each day for a week, Mary goes outside for a short time, three minutes. She just stands outside the door and practises a few deep breaths and relaxing. She walks calmly back in.

- In week two she does the same again, but this time gets as far as the gate. She gets used to being out in the fresh air.

- In week three Mary decides to walk calmly outside and this time she takes 10 steps away from the gate, then walks back in. In addition she spends three minutes each evening just stood outside the front door breathing calmly, concentrating on breathing out the black feeling of anxiety and breathing back in pure air, thinking of it as golden coloured and soothing. She decides that, through the rest of the steps in her plan, she will carry on doing this, standing outside each day for three minutes as well. It makes her feel like more of an outdoor type of person.

- In week four Mary decides that she might need a little extra help so she asks her daughter if she will come with her to the end of the road on the first couple of days. Then, the rest of the week she asks her daughter if she will just stand at the gate so that she can see her walking to the end of the road and back.

- In week five, Mary walks to the end of the road and back each day. She imagines she is breathing out the black anxiety as she goes along, and she sees herself breathing in golden air to make her strong. She deliberately adopts a good upright posture. She takes her mobile phone with her and she has her daughter on speed dial, but her daughter is not there because she has asked her to be back in Mary's house making a cup of tea for when she returns.

- In week six, Mary walks to the end of the road and back. She does not ask her daughter to be there, although she still makes sure she takes her mobile phone with her.

- In week seven, Mary decides it would be a good thing to be a bit fitter. She carries on walking to the end of the road and back each day, and her three minutes outside the door each evening. However, in addition she practises some exercises at home, running on the spot for a minute, with a plan to build on that over the next few weeks.

- In week eight, Mary and her daughter walk halfway to the shops together. This means walking along three streets and her house is not in sight. They walk back home and Mary concentrates on calm breathing.

- In week nine, Mary does the same distance but her daughter is back at her house waiting for her return. Mary makes sure she has her mobile phone with her.

- In week 10, Mary walks to the shops. Her daughter walks behind her, but out of sight. She arrives at the shops as Mary finishes making her purchase. They walk home together.

- In week 11, Mary walks to the shops and back by herself.

You can see that this series of 11 graded stages sees Mary achieving her first goal within 11 weeks. She has planned out the steps before she even starts on week one.

For your own particular fear, write out a series of graded stages that will get you to a major goal in around three months. Of course, every person's list will be different. Try to tailor your plan to your own requirements.

Don't become dependent on someone to help you, but if you can use someone you trust to help you over a big hurdle, then do that. Mary was pleased to have her daughter help out with some parts of her plan, but at the same time she realised that she could not simply rely on her daughter to be there all the time.

This example gets Mary to a major goal for her. She carries on going out, but realises that it is important to vary where she goes. So she draws up another series of steps to get her to her next big goal, going out further into town on a bus. She uses the same strategy as before of a series of mini goals that are not too big, and using her daughter for support for some of the time.

Adapting the plan

Before you start to work your way down the steps in your plan, it is best to really think through all the stages and to write them down in your notebook.

In Mary's example she took a week for each stage. You decide on the time for each of your stages. It might be that some are shorter, just a couple of days, and for some stages in the plan you may need longer to adjust, but aim for no longer than 10-14 days at any stage.

Of course it is possible that you will become stuck on a particular stage. After all you have thought through your plan, but it is very theoretical and in practice you might find that some of your stages are too big. Should that happen, then just add an extra stage.

For example, when Mary planned out the stages to her goal she originally had 10 stages. However, after week eight she had planned walking to the shops for week nine but that was just too difficult for her. So she made up a new stage, as described in week nine. That helped her, gave her a bridge to getting to the shops by herself which then became week 10.

Remember that you are your own best guide here. You want to make yourself a little anxious with each stage, but your aim is to master that stage.

Breathing deeply a few times can help. Do not forget the things you learnt in the last chapter and use these new skills to help you should you feel anxious when doing your task for the week.

Continue to keep your notebook to record your progress. Write down how you feel when you accomplish each step and keep dates of your progress.

If you suffer a setback do not get down about it. Drop back a stage if you need to, and think about adding little additional steps to build you to the next stage.

Modelling

It can be very helpful, especially for some fears, if you can see someone you trust 'modelling' the behaviour that you want to achieve.

For example, if you have a fear of spiders, your stages to goal might start very simply (so you just say the word spider and picture it in your mind). Your stages might build up so that you see pictures of spiders, see spiders at the zoo, see spiders in a film. Eventually you might have a friend show you a tiny spider in a jar, at the other end of the room to you. Eventually, over the stages, they come closer so that you might hold the jar. You work your way up to having the spider on your hand.

Now this might take many weeks to achieve and along the way you will learn to relax and feel the anxiety go from you as you calmly breathe out your anxiety.

If you have a friend who is not fearful of spiders, at the stage where there is the small spider in the jar, that friend could model how you want to behave. The friend could take the spider out of the jar and let it go on their hand. All you have to do is observe from the other side of the room. Go closer as you feel your anxiety ebb away.

The power of imagination

Try, at least once each day, to do your relaxation exercises and, when you are comfortable and calm, picture yourself going through your actions, the particular stage you are on at any one time.

For Mary, not only did she actually go out each day, in bed at night before she went to sleep she did her relaxation exercises and then imagined herself going outside. She relived what she did during the day. She pictured herself as calm and confident and accomplishing what she set out to achieve.

Before trying the next stage she would also imagine herself doing it first, doing it and achieving what she wanted.

It is very important for you to imagine the thing you are anxious about, see yourself doing the thing you fear and imagine yourself relaxing as you do it. Very often, people will deliberately block thoughts about the thing that worries them. They therefore never give themselves a chance to adapt to it.

The more you try to suppress a negative thought the more power it will have over you. So, welcome in your fearful thoughts and learn to turn the fear off in your mind and replace it with positive thoughts. Breathe anxiety out and imagine yourself as a success, someone who can cope.

Imagination and action

Some of the stages in your plan could be based on you imagining what you will be doing to face your fear.

For example, if you have a fear of travelling on a bus or flying in a plane, there are some practical hurdles to be overcome before you can attempt a journey. Your hierarchy of stages might start with you looking at pictures of buses or planes. If you fear flying then one stage might include a visit to an airport. But at some point in your plan you are going to have to get on board and travel.

Before that point you can use your imagination. Have a stage where you picture yourself getting on board. Do this after you are very relaxed.

▥ Vividly imagine the scene.

▥ Think to yourself 'how anxious am I now on a scale of 1 to 10?'

▥ Even if your anxiety is really high, stay with the scene and slowly and carefully breathe away your anxiety.

▥ After five minutes re-rate your anxiety. It will be lower.

▥ Keep rehearsing the feared scene and counter any anxiety by doing your breathing, letting the black anxiety out of your body.

▥ After about 10 or 15 minutes you will find your anxiety level has dropped significantly.

■ Stay relaxed, feel your muscles warm and heavy.

Repeat this over a few occasions until you feel in control of your body when you imagine the scene. You can try the same technique with different scenes associated with the thing that you fear. So the next stage might be you imagining getting on board and experiencing the start of the journey. Finally, you imagine yourself doing the whole journey in a completely relaxed manner.

In the next chapter we shall see that what is also important is your thinking style. The actual words going through your head are only words, but they have the power to change your emotions.

To be really successful at overcoming anxiety you will learn to put together all the elements, so you can relax, stop avoiding things, use your imagination, and change the way you think, change the actual words that are running through your mind and feel calm.

Summing Up

It is no good to avoid the thing that makes you anxious as you will never learn to overcome your fear of it. Come up with a plan, a series of graded steps that will see you to your goal. Learn to relax as you expose yourself to anxiety-provoking situations. Also practise imagining yourself doing these tasks, relaxing and succeeding.

It's important to keep a record of your progress and add additional little steps inbetween if you need to. Get a friend to help out if you can, but don't become reliant on them. A good friend can model the kinds of action that you are aiming for. Once you have gone through your steps and achieved your goal, think of further goals you might like to aim for to broaden your horizons even more.

Chapter Eight

Change Your Thoughts

Negative thoughts and anxiety

What does it mean to be anxious? Anxiety is a very complex problem. We have seen that you need to be able to counter anxiety by relaxing your body. You also need a plan of action and graded exposure to the thing you fear, so you are no longer avoiding whatever makes you anxious.

However, one of the notable things about anxious people is what they think, the words that they rehearse in their mind.

Anxious people always imagine the worst. They catastrophize and see danger lurking. This happens almost irrespective of what they are anxious about.

Let us think back to Martha's anxiety that we discussed in chapters 4 and 5. Her worry is about her children. She worries about their safety and wellbeing. Although it is good to care, Martha now worries about them all the time, if they are away or if they are at home.

So, as the children leave the house in the morning this is what Martha thinks and does:

- 'This could be the day they die.'
- 'Will I get a phone call or would the police come round to tell me they have been in an accident?'
- 'I'll take my mind off it by cleaning the house.'
- 'I had better check they have unplugged the TV in their bedroom or else there could be a fire' (Martha checks and rechecks through the day).
- 'This meal could give them food poisoning.'

'One of the notable things about anxious people is what they think, the words that they rehearse in their mind.'

- 'Germs could make them seriously ill if I don't clean.'

- Martha spends the day cleaning and worrying.

When the children come home safe that does not make the anxiety fade, because now new dangers lurk. After cooking tea she goes back into the kitchen at regular intervals to see if the gas is off. She fears that it might come through to where they are watching TV, they might all doze off to sleep, then the gas will kill them. Finally, it takes her at least an hour each night to get to bed because she checks and rechecks the lights are off, plugs are out of sockets and the gas is off.

She sees disaster everywhere. She cannot relax. Her emotions run high and she feels continuously stressed and nervous.

We have seen that it is important that she stops her checking and seeking reassurance; she has to stop texting her children to see if they are alright when out of the home. She can make a plan of action and do it over time, she can also learn to breathe deeply and relax.

But she will benefit the most if she can also change her thoughts.

What are your thoughts that are associated with your particular anxiety? Are you someone that imagines the worst?

You might even think that you have managed to keep disaster at bay by imagining the worst. You picture the worst happening every day, and it has not happened. Maybe that is a way to keep things safe?

If you think that, then I want you to seriously evaluate just how unlikely that is. How could thinking the worst keep anyone safe? You will find that you have let yourself slip into strange ways of thinking that have become a habit. Fortunately habits can be broken:

- Take some time to write down in your notebook your typical thoughts, the thoughts that accompany your anxiety.

- Try to imagine different scenarios and write down the thoughts that would accompany each.

- Write next to each thought the kind of emotion you have when you have that thought.

That is a picture of your mental life. How happy are you with it?

Rate each thought for how likely it is

For each of your thoughts rate out of 100 just how likely it is.

To give you some idea of how to rate, this is how Martha rates her thoughts.

- She rates 'this could be the day they die' as 70, really quite likely.

- If she does not check the TV plugs are out of the sockets she rates the thought 'there will be a fire' as 90.

- She rates 'this food might poison them' as 70.

- If she does not clean all day she rates her thought 'the children will become ill through germs' as 95.

- The thought 'we might all be gassed unless I check the oven' she rates as 80.

She sees doom everywhere and, furthermore, she realises as she rates these thoughts that she thinks disaster is very likely.

Do you see disaster associated with your particular anxiety? How realistic is it to think this way?

Challenge your thoughts

Consider each one of your thoughts in turn and break it into smaller pieces. For example, Martha looks at the thought 'this food might poison them' and she breaks it down into a set of smaller events:

- The food being contaminated before it enters the house.

- The food becoming contaminated once in her fridge.

- The food not being cooked enough and poisonous.

She rates each of these three points in turn. She thinks the chances of food being contaminated when it is quite fresh, before it even arrives at her house, as low, a rating of 15 out of 100.

She always keeps the fridge at a good temperature and always cooks the food by the date suggested on the packet. So she thinks the chances of the food going bad in the fridge is also low, about 10 out of 100.

She thinks her cooking is pretty good so really the chances of poisoning at that stage is only about 10 out of 100 as well.

So, looking at this logically, she can see that she was probably overestimating danger when she rated her initial single thought 'this food might poison them' as 70.

She re-rates her score for 'this food might poison them' as more like 10 out of 100 for now.

You can see the kind of process involved in challenging your thoughts. As well as trying to think things through, you can also challenge yourself with little experiments. Think back to the last chapter when Mary was frightened of going outdoors. One of her thoughts was 'if I go out I will faint with fear' and she rated this highly. But she built her plan of action, she started slow with it, and she realised that going outside would not make her faint.

What if the worst does happen?

Bad things do happen, but far less often than anxious people think they will. However, on rare occasions, things do not go as well as you want them to.

Mostly people cope far better than they think they will. For example, with Martha, if the children did get food poisoning, the odds are overwhelming that they would recover. If she left the gas on, chances are that someone would smell it and then turn the gas tap off.

However, sometimes bad things happen. You worry you might have cancer and you find you have it. Or a loved one dies. Or you lose your job. Major negative life events happen to everyone, irrespective of whether they spend their lives feeling highly anxious.

'It is a sad waste of your time to live in a state of anxiety and high emotion. When the bad thing happens you will find you have resources to cope. Friends rally round or you learn slowly to accept what has happened. You readjust your life to your new circumstances. In fact, you will readjust better and faster if you are the kind of person who is positive in outlook and not negative and anxiety ridden.

You might as well look on the bright side – it will help you to cope with life's ups and downs.

'It is a sad waste of your time to live in a state of anxiety and high emotion. When the bad thing happens you will find you have resources to cope.'

Need2Know

When you need a major life change to get rid of anxiety

Earlier we saw that Ben was feeling anxious about his job. He confided in too many people and he thinks they now think of him as a loser. He sent off too many complaining emails, started drinking and being moody at home.

He certainly can learn relaxation techniques. He can also consider changing aspects of his behaviour at work. He can cut back on his drinking and try to find pleasure with being with his family. However, he might still find he has an issue with the job itself. Sometimes major change is needed in order to be happy. He might need to start searching for other employment.

To take another example, if you feel general anxiety most of the time, you can counteract it. You can learn to relax, learn to challenge your thoughts, but it might be that there is something fundamental that needs changing. Are you bored at home? Are you happy with your marriage? Do you need a new challenge in life?

These are issues that are personal to each individual. Only you can really reflect on your life. You have to be honest with yourself and also realistic. Big changes are difficult to make, so give yourself time to try out various routes to an end goal that will make a significant difference. Expect to fail at some of the alternative solutions that you try. Don't get upset if you go for a job and don't get it. Get feedback on your performance, learn from it, and retry. If in the end you don't get offered a new job, what else in life might be interesting for you? Maybe a new hobby or taking an evening course might be the answer. You have to put yourself out there to be in with a chance of finding new and interesting experiences.

Don't be afraid of your anxiety

Sometimes people become afraid of the anxiety itself. If they get anxious they feel a failure. They worry that the anxiety itself might overwhelm them. They tie themselves in knots over this.

Remember, quite simply, that:

- Everyone gets anxious at times.
- You have the power to control your anxiety.
- Counteract tension by relaxing.
- Breathe deeply.
- Rate and challenge those negative thoughts.
- Draw up a plan of action.
- Don't avoid the thing that frightens you.
- Don't seek reassurance all the time.
- Act confident, feel confident, be confident.

The state of anxiety does not descend on you out of nowhere. It is a physical state you can change. It comes with thoughts that you can alter.

Be positive

Don't let any day go by without mentally rehearsing some positive things. Here are some ideas to get you going:

- The happiest birthday you have had.
- Things that make you laugh.
- Your best holiday.
- The kindest person you know.
- Things you love to do.
- The best films you have seen.
- Your favourite book or author.
- Your favourite clothes.
- The nicest meal ever.
- People you are grateful to.

There are many things that you can feel positive about. You have a store of happy memories inside of you and you can tap into them every day. Really dwell on your topic of choice for the day. Make plans about how to increase your happiness rather than simply dwelling on how to rid yourself of anxiety.

Summing Up

You have power over your thoughts. Reflect on the thoughts that are related to your anxiety and you will find that you catastrophize: you fear the worst and you are likely to rate the probability of disaster as far higher than the true chances.

You can learn to challenge your beliefs and become more realistic. Even if the worst does happen you will find that you can cope. You can adapt to life's ups and downs. Think about the big changes you can make to enjoy life more.

Don't be afraid of your anxiety, understand that everyone is anxious from time to time. You can learn to control anxiety in a way that you like and that you are comfortable with. Reflect on positive thoughts every day.

'You can adapt
to life's ups
and downs.'

Need2Know

Chapter Nine

Keep Healthy

Food and drink

Very often when faced with anxiety we have seen that people seek instant relief. They avoid the feared object. They seek reassurance. They develop little rituals that they find comforting.

You can learn to change all of those things as we have seen throughout this book. That way, you will be able to rid yourself of the high anxiety that makes you unhappy.

However, it is also the case that anxiety can lead to very unhealthy behaviours. In our examples from earlier, Ben started to drink heavily on a daily basis, and Martha started to eat a lot more.

People often turn to food and drink as a comfort. In a way that is something we all do and it can be adaptive if done in the right way. A hot cup of tea can be very soothing for instance. Drinking copious cups of strong tea or coffee is likely to have the opposite effect and you will become quite jittery and have sleep problems.

'Anxiety can lead to very unhealthy behaviours.'

Excessive consumption

The danger comes when people do things to excess. If you drink alcohol through the evening you are quite likely to feel your heart pounding a few hours later. As you lie in bed you might feel it pounding against the mattress. You sweat. You feel you are getting palpitations. In fact, the effect of the alcohol is similar to a panic reaction. You have accidently created a physical sensation that is akin to severe anxiety.

Drinking outside of the safe limit (two units a day for a woman, three units for a man) is likely to increase your feelings of anxiety. It is important for both your mental and physical health to drink within sensible limits.

Don't fool yourself about how much you drink.

- A large glass of wine is not one unit. A large glass is more likely to be between three and four units.

- A pint of beer or lager might be about two units if it is weak (around or just under 4% strength). But most beer is stronger and a pint can be more like three units or even as high as five or six units.

- A measure of spirits is usually one unit but often bars give generous measures which will therefore be more than a single unit.

- Know your drink, look up the units on the bottle and be on the safe side when you make your calculations.

'If you do something positive for yourself, apply a little self care, you will feel better about yourself.'

If you binge-drink, generally six or more units in one go, you are more than likely to have sleep disturbance. Typically you might wake early in the morning and find it difficult to go back to sleep.

This is likely to make you more anxious and possibly depressed if it goes on long term. So seeking solace in alcohol is counterproductive. It will make your anxiety worse in the long term.

Eating too much might feel comforting, but becoming overweight is not likely to make you feel better about yourself and you will be unhappy if none of your clothes fit.

Some people try to cope with anxiety by taking tight control of their food intake. They go to the opposite extreme, become too thin or even develop anorexia or bulimia.

Develop a healthy body

If you do something positive for yourself, apply a little self-care, you will feel better about yourself. The higher your self-esteem the more likely it is you will be a confident and successful person who can tackle their fears.

90

It is therefore very important that you give yourself achievable goals that will lead to increased health.

Pick things that are right for you.

Diet

In terms of diet, there is no need to be too radical. Try to go with the guidelines that encourage you to:

- Eat more fruit and vegetables, try to eat your 5-a-day.
- Consume less saturated fat.
- Have fewer sugary foods.
- Eat less processed foods.
- Cut down on salt.
- Eat more lean protein.
- Enjoy nuts and pulses.
- Try some soya products.
- Have oily fish a couple of times a week.
- Choose low fat dairy products, skimmed or semi-skimmed rather than full fat.
- Have wholegrain bread, rice and pasta, rather than white versions.
- Have healthy oils, like olive oil, rather than hard fat.

Have some sweet things as occasional treats but feel you are nurturing your body on a daily basis. Get interested in recipe books, try cooking with different herbs. Think about food in a positive way.

Even with your treats you can find fun indulging yourself. If you fancy a bit of chocolate, learn something about it. If you join a chocolate club you can find out all sorts of interesting things about the product.

- Don't feel guilty about eating.
- Enjoy your food.

- Try to follow your natural appetite and if you fancy something, have it.

- Eat slowly.

- Eat when you are hungry and when you start to feel full then stop, even if it means leaving something on your plate.

If you are overweight, think long term. A loss of a single pound of fat a month soon mounts up, it even comes to almost a stone in a year. After three years, losing a single pound every month will mean you would be two and a half stones lighter. That would solve many people's weight problems. You will not be hungry if you lose at such a slow rate. Draw a graph with an 'aim line' pencilled in and try to keep to it. Sometimes you might be just above the line, sometimes just below, but try to be roughly on the line until you reach goal.

For more information about healthy eating and weight loss, see *Food for Health – The Essential Guide* and *Weight Loss – The Essential Guide* (Need2Know).

Exercise

Exercise is really an essential part of any person's life. Pick something that is right for you. For example:

- If you like company, join a gym, take up a team sport or join a running or walking club.

- If you want to build exercise into your life in a more natural way, then walk more instead of using your car and take the stairs instead of the lift.

- If you like to exercise at home, try a home exercise DVD.

There are countless things you could try.

As you exercise you will feel your heart rate increase in a perfectly natural way. You will see it is something that is healthy. The rate goes up to meet the demand of exercise, and then it naturally goes back down again. You will be able to observe your own body when it is responding as it should. You will learn to trust your body to carry you through whatever life throws at you.

You might even want to expand your knowledge about relaxation. Some types of exercise are very calming for the mind. Maybe you would like to try yoga or T'ai chi.

Smoking

Giving up cigarettes is one of the hardest things, but luckily it has never been easier than now. Nicotine patches and gum are available and your chemist or GP will be able to give you advice.

The main thing will be that you have to be self-motivated. Stopping smoking is something that only you can decide to do.

If you smoke only occasionally or if you smoke very little you should be able to give up all in one go. That also works for heavy smokers too. Pick a day on which you are going to be a non-smoker, make up your mind, and stop.

However, if you have tried it and found it impossible, do what you have learnt to do in overcoming anxiety. Draw up a plan. Make it one that you think you can follow. If you smoke 30 cigarettes a day you could, for instance, reduce that by five a month until you are on 10 a day. Stay with that amount for a couple of months then cut them out altogether. Use nicotine patches or gum as necessary. That is one plan of action. It is up to you to make up your own plan to suit your life and your level of motivation.

Visit your GP for advice on how to stop smoking.

Health and social activity

Generally, you will find it easier to be healthy if you make it fun. Joining in with other people or getting family members involved is likely to keep you motivated long term. Human beings are social creatures and you will get more pleasure out of life if you share your interests with others.

Summing Up

Leading a healthy life will increase your confidence and decrease your feelings of anxiety. It is particularly important that you do not seek comfort by drinking excessive amounts of alcohol or caffeine.

It is easy to get to a good weight if you take a slow approach over months or even over a few years. Concentrate on your enjoyment of food and learn how to eat in a healthy, fun way.

Take up exercise, give up smoking if you need to. Make your new healthier lifestyle one you share with others.

Chapter Ten

Family and Friends

You do not exist in isolation. You may have parents. You may well have brothers, sisters, cousins, aunts and uncles. You may have children and they may have their own children. You can, and should, use these people as a source of joy, support, a fund of happy memories. Or you can use them as a source of anxiety.

You have choices and the power to make the right choices.

Your children

We have seen that anxious people often feel very responsible for those around them. For example, a mother might feel heavily responsible for the care of her children:

▪ When she is pregnant there is the possibility of miscarriage.

▪ Will the birth be normal?

▪ What are the chances of cot death?

▪ Will they like school?

▪ Will they have a traffic accident?

▪ Will they get out of control as teenagers?

▪ Will they do well at school?

▪ Can I afford to support them at university?

▪ Will they get a job?

The fact of the matter is you can spend a lifetime worrying about your children and it will be to no avail. You are not responsible for every little thing that happens to them. There will be lots of things that you cannot control and that is the fact of it. It is better to mentally let go of the worry and concentrate on the here and now and the joy of the moment.

The older generation

If you think about the other end of the scale, those older than you, parents and grandparents, it is very likely that they will fall ill from time to time. One day, you will probably have to go to their funeral.

Now, on the face of it, that is a depressing and very sad thought. If you decide to cling on to such thoughts, get anxious and gloomy about it, you will be living a very unhappy life day on day, year on year.

- It is very important that you learn to let go of what you cannot control.

'Learn to let go of what you cannot control.'

- Life has a natural rhythm and you have to accept that fact.
- Every moment you spend thinking negative thoughts is a waste if it does not bring about positive change. You are far better off concentrating on the here and now.
- Think about all the happy moments that your family bring you.
- Plan out ways to make them happy, little treats or surprises.
- Share your pleasures with them as much as you can.
- Take an interest in their life, their friends, but don't be overbearing.
- Be there when you're needed, if you can be.
- Remember that people who love you want you to be happy and they want you to think of them in happy ways.

Your friends and community

Whether you have lots of family or hardly any at all, you still have a social network. Each person comes into contact with others.

96

Try to find others with similar interests and join in.

Just being around others, or having a drink in a café alone and looking at people, can help you feel a part of the wider community.

You can have lots of people you know in passing, share the odd conversation with. But try to keep up with old friends, and have at least one or two that you consider to be really close. As well as meeting up there are lots of social networking sites and it is easy to keep in touch.

Try to give something back to the community. Small things, like becoming a blood donor, can give you a sense of belonging.

Don't just think of what your friends can do for you, think about what you can do for them. Be prepared to listen, to make yourself available for them.

If you concentrate on others in a caring and loving way then your worries about yourself will fade into the background. You will feel part of a bigger community. You will be happy.

Keeping on top of your anxiety

If you read this book and follow the advice you will find that you learn to conquer your anxiety. You will have been thinking about your current anxiety problems and will have used the techniques described to help yourself overcome them.

Although you have learnt to tackle what is bothering you right now, it is inevitable that new challenges will present themselves as you go along life's way.

You have learnt to overcome your present anxiety problems and you can tackle future problems too. In fact, you should feel much more confident in your ability to control your thoughts and emotions, keep your body relaxed and have a self-confident and positive outlook on life.

So, do not be surprised the next time you feel anxious. Remember to:

▨ Practise your relaxation technique on a daily basis in the privacy of your own home.

▨ Relax when faced with a stressful situation or thought.

'Keep your body relaxed, and have a self-confident and positive outlook on life.'

- Challenge your negative thoughts and take a rational view of them.

- Make an action plan to tackle your anxiety problem head on.

If you ensure that you nurture your relationships, have family and good friends that you can rely on as a part of your social network, you will find it much easier to adapt to the ups and downs that are an inevitable part of life.

Concentrate more on the positive aspects of being alive. Don't let negative thoughts take over. Don't expect catastrophe to happen at every turn. Don't avoid issues that make you anxious. Finally, remember that, whatever happens, you have the resources within you to cope with adversity and to lead a happy life.

'You have the resources within you to cope.'

Summing Up

Family and friends are a very important thing in anyone's life. Of course there is the potential for them to be a source of anxiety. If you care deeply about someone it is natural that you want the best for them. It is natural that you want them to be around. However, you have to accept that their wellbeing is not a responsibility that you can shoulder all alone. Some things are uncontrollable.

We are all part of the circle of life. If you build a sense of belonging, if you concentrate on the positive aspects of social interaction, you will find your anxiety will be controlled and you will be a happier person.

Help List

Alcohol Concern

64, Leman Street, London, E1 8EU
Tel: 0800 917 8282 (helpline)
www.alcoholconcern.org.uk
Alcohol Concern gives information about alcohol and also gives access to a services directory so you can access local services in England and Wales.

Anxiety UK

Zion CRC, 339, Stretford Road, Hulme, Manchester, M15 4ZY
Tel: 08444 775 774 (helpline)
info@anxietyuk.org.uk
www.anxietyuk.org.uk
Anxiety UK is a national charity which gives information, support and advice on the whole range of anxiety disorders.

BBC

www.bbc.co.uk/health/emotional_health
This BBC page provides information about a wide range of emotional problems including the anxiety disorders, coping skills, self-confidence issues and relaxation.

British Psychological Society

St. Andrew's House, 48, Princess Road East, Leicester, LE1 7DR
Tel: 0116 254 9568
enquiries@bps.org.uk
www.bps.org.uk
There is a 'find a psychologist' section on the British Psychological Society's website that allows you to locate a therapist in your area.

Drinkaware

Samuel House, 6 St Albans St, London, SW1Y 4SQ
Tel: 020 7766 9900
www.drinkaware.co.uk
This gives useful information on units that allows you to calculate your alcohol intake. It gives information on a wide range of alcohol-related behaviours, such as drinking on medication and binge drinking.

Food Doctor

www.thefooddoctor.com
This website gives good nutritional advice, including how to lose weight. There is a range of books available by Ian Marber, that give information about everyday diet and how to lose weight.

Helpguide.org

www.helpguide.org
Helpguide.org gives information related to mental and emotional health and active healthy lifestyles.

International Stress Management Association UK

PO Box 491, Bradley, Stoke, Bristol, BS34 9AH
www.isma.org.uk
ISMA gives information about prevention, reduction and management of personal and work-related stress.

Mind

Tel: 0845 766 0163 (helpline)
www.mind.org.uk
This is a well-established organisation that gives information about mental health issues. It also gives you links to local Mind associations in your area. If requested it will send printed information.

National Drugs Helpline / Talk to Frank

Tel: 0800 77 66 00 (helpline)
Text: 82111
www.talktofrank.com
This provides information about drugs and also a 24-hour free and confidential helpline.

OCD-UK

PO Box 8955, Nottingham, NG10 9AU
www.ocduk.org
This is a leading national charity working with and for people with obsessive-compulsive disorder. It gives information about OCD at different ages, how to help yourself and also how to find a therapist. There are support group contacts in England, Scotland and Wales, and these groups run independently of OCD-UK.

Patient UK

www.patient.co.uk
This site gives health information about a comprehensive range of physical problems as well as anxiety-related issues in the mental health category.

Relate

Tel: 0300 100 1234 (helpline)
www.relate.org.uk
This is a counselling service for couples but also for individuals about family-related matters.

Social Anxiety Organisation

www.social-anxiety.org.uk
This website gives diagnostic criteria, information and resources and includes chat rooms.

Need - 2 - Know

Available Titles Include ...

Allergies A Parent's Guide
ISBN 978-1-86144-064-8 £8.99

Autism A Parent's Guide
ISBN 978-1-86144-069-3 £8.99

Blood Pressure The Essential Guide
ISBN 978-1-86144-067-9 £8.99

Dyslexia and Other Learning Difficulties
A Parent's Guide ISBN 978-1-86144-042-6 £8.99

Bullying A Parent's Guide
ISBN 978-1-86144-044-0 £8.99

Epilepsy The Essential Guide
ISBN 978-1-86144-063-1 £8.99

Your First Pregnancy The Essential Guide
ISBN 978-1-86144-066-2 £8.99

Gap Years The Essential Guide
ISBN 978-1-86144-079-2 £8.99

Secondary School A Parent's Guide
ISBN 978-1-86144-093-8 £9.99

Primary School A Parent's Guide
ISBN 978-1-86144-088-4 £9.99

Applying to University The Essential Guide
ISBN 978-1-86144-052-5 £8.99

ADHD The Essential Guide
ISBN 978-1-86144-060-0 £8.99

Student Cookbook – Healthy Eating The Essential Guide
ISBN 978-1-86144-069-3 £8.99

Multiple Sclerosis The Essential Guide
ISBN 978-1-86144-086-0 £8.99

Coeliac Disease The Essential Guide
ISBN 978-1-86144-087-7 £9.99

Special Educational Needs A Parent's Guide
ISBN 978-1-86144-116-4 £9.99

The Pill An Essential Guide
ISBN 978-1-86144-058-7 £8.99

University A Survival Guide
ISBN 978-1-86144-072-3 £8.99

View the full range at **www.need2knowbooks.co.uk**.
To order our titles call **01733 898103**, email **sales@
n2kbooks.com** or visit the website. Selected ebooks
available online.

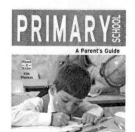

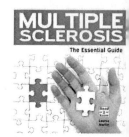

Need - 2 - Know, Remus House, Coltsfoot Drive, Peterborough, PE2 9BF